TURBULENT TIMES FOR THE SOVIET CHURCH

The Inside Story

KENT R. HILL

MULTNOMAH

Portland, Oregon
in cooperation with the
Institute on Religion and Democracy

To my parents,

D. E. and Helen Hill;

models of love and service to others.

TURBULENT TIMES FOR THE SOVIET CHURCH
©1991 by Kent R. Hill
Published by Multnomah Press
10209 SE Division Street
Portland, Oregon 97266
in cooperation with the Institute on Religion and Democracy
Washington, D.C. 20005

Multnomah Press is a ministry of Multnomah School of the Bible,
8435 NE Glisan Street, Portland, Oregon 97220.

Cover design by Durand Demlow
Edited by Al Janssen and Rodney L. Morris

Printed in the United States of America.

Library of Congress Cataloging-in-Publication Data

Hill, Kent Richmond.
    Turbulent times for the Soviet church / Kent R. Hill.
      p.   cm.
      ISBN 0-88070-462-4
      1. Soviet Union—Church history—1917- 2. Church and state—Soviet Union—History—1917- 3. Communism and Christianity—Soviet Union—History. I. Title.
BR936.H56   1991
323.44'2'0947—dc20   91-20337
                                                                              CIP

91 92 93 94 95 96 97 98 99 00 - 10 9 8 7 6 5 4 3 2 1

CONTENTS

INTRODUCTION

*T*urmoil and uncertainty dominate the Soviet landscape. The euphoria over the early days of Mikhail Gorbachev and glasnost, especially in the West, is steadily giving way to a more sober, even ominous foreboding about the future.

By the spring of 1991, massive pro-democracy demonstrations calling for Gorbachev's resignation were being held within the shadow of the Kremlin. An increasingly large military presence in the very heart of Moscow raised the specter of Tiananmen Square—the bloody Chinese crackdown on reformists in 1989. Beyond fears of government attacks on its critics, there is now open talk in the Soviet Union of the possibility of civil war.

Images of violence in the Baltics, Caucasus, and Central Asia tumble across our TV screens, testifying to deep ethnic and nationalist divisions in the Soviet empire. Whether the Soviet Union can, or should, continue to exist is very much in question. *Glasnost* and democratization have always been incompatible with the continuation of the Union of Soviet Socialist Republics—an involuntary union including captive nationalities. But so far *glasnost*, not the union, is giving way,

Utterly empty store shelves testify to the bankruptcy of the Marxist economic experiment, and *perestroika* has not arrested the slide toward Third World poverty. "You can't eat *glasnost*," as one cynical Russian put it.

The demise or retreat of Marxism as an ideology is no guarantee of the rise of democracy to take its place. Given the Russian historical tendency toward authoritarianism, insecurity will play into the hands of those who insist that a "strong hand" is needed to bring order out of chaos.

But the growing instability of recent months ought not blind us to the stunning changes which have occurred since Gorbachev took power in 1985. *Glasnost*, the deliberate policy of more honestly dealing with both past and present, was not a clever propaganda ploy. It was and is real, and the Soviet Union can never be the same again. Many crimes of the past, including numerous ones committed by the Communist party itself, have been acknowledged. Long forbidden authors such as Solzhenitsyn have been published. Numerous publications, and even television, reflect a variety of opinions previously not allowed in the public square. The constitutional guarantee of a monopoly of power for the Communists has been abolished. The relative advantages of a market economy over a state-controlled economy has been noted and debated, but no workable plan for implementation is yet in place.

There can be little doubt that the motive for the Gorbachev "openness" was to reform communism, not abolish it, but the forces unleashed have almost certainly made a return to totalitarianism impossible. Communism may remain an attractive ideology for some Western radicals, but not for the vast majority of the citizens of Communist or formerly Communist lands.

Totalitarian instruments of power and coercion continue to exist, and it is no simple task to dismantle the institutions and structures which have provided, and continue to provide, power and privileges to those who have the most to lose from fundamental change.

Outside the borders of the Soviet Union, Eastern Europe as a satellite Communist empire has ceased to exist. The Warsaw Pact has been disbanded, the Berlin Wall has been smashed, and East Germany has been absorbed into West Germany. The Romanian dictator Nicolae Ceausescu was swept from power and then executed, while Communist rulers in Bulgaria, Czechoslovakia, Hungary, and Yugoslavia either have lost power or are losing it. Even Albania is being rocked by calls for change. Communism is not dead but it is in retreat, and it was Gorbachev's renunciation of the use of force to prop up these regimes which unintentionally opened the floodgates. But the self-determination he has reluctantly allowed for the countries of Eastern Europe he seems determined not to permit for the republics of the Soviet Union.

Religion is much freer in the Soviet Union in 1991 than it was in

1985. The vast majority of prisoners who were incarcerated for religious reasons have been released. For several years, particularly beginning in 1987, the oppressive laws restricting religious activities were not enforced. Churches were allowed openly to engage in charity, to evangelize, to import and in some cases print large quantities of Bibles and religious literature, to reopen some closed churches, to begin to provide modest religious training for their children, and to have more internal control over their own affairs.

The authorities allowed major public celebrations of the millennium anniversary of the coming of Orthodox Christianity to the Eastern Slavs. Public and media references to religion and churches have been decidedly more positive than in the pre-Gorbachev era, and there has even been considerable public acknowledgement of past discrimination and persecution of believers by the government. State interference in church affairs has also been confessed and condemned.

In October 1991, the USSR Freedom of Conscience Law was finally adopted. It formally abolished the above-noted restrictions on religious faith which had existed in legal statutes since 1929. The registration of religious communities, however, was not eliminated, though currently the more sinister efforts to control the church through registration do not seem to be present. The law provides for continuing some sort of government liaison body with religious groups, and for many this is a cause for concern. The Council for Religious Affairs, after all, has traditionally not been an organ of liaison but of control and intervention.

The most stunning clause in the new law is Article 5: "The state does not fund religious organizations or activity associated with the propaganda of atheism." For decades the Soviet state has invested millions of rubles and unleashed a virtual army of government-funded, militantly antireligious propagandists to preach the Marxist message of atheism in the public schools. Such expenditures of funds and influence are now illegal.

Many analysts of Soviet society, both inside and outside the USSR, observe that Marxist communism has had a devastating impact on societal morals. The much touted new "Soviet man," which communism sought so hard to fashion, has failed to materialize. On the contrary, crime is skyrocketing. There is massive evidence that systematic lying has become a way of life for millions.

Indeed, the heart of the Soviet Union's problems is spiritual, not political or economic. This makes the mission of the church all the more urgent, for a vibrant faith can provide the values, the courage, the hope, the patience, and the meaning necessary to build a new society based on truth rather than falsehood.

The profound moral crisis, when combined with the increasingly dangerous economic and political situation, spawns gloomy prognostications about the future. And yet the edge of despair can also be the threshold of hope. At least this is always the case wherever the gospel is present, and there is probably no mission field in the world as open as that of the Soviet Union and other countries where the emptiness of atheist communism is present for all to see.

People in the Soviet Union are in quest of a soul. But it must never be forgotten that Christianity is not foreign to many of the peoples of the USSR. The Armenians and Georgians have been influenced by Orthodoxy since at least the fourth century, Catholicism has been extremely important in Lithuania and the Western Ukraine for centuries, Lutheranism has been a significant influence in the Baltics, and Orthodoxy for over a thousand years has been a dominant force in Slavic culture.

Soviet communism sought to excise religion from the individual and collective memories of the peoples under its iron grip. But despite great persecution, Christianity and other religions have survived, though religious organizations have been badly damaged. The severe lack of religious literature, trained clergy, and proper facilities are problems endemic to virtually all religious bodies. In addition, there is the problem of the seriously compromised senior religious leadership. Where spiritual renewal is taking place, it rarely is something which originates at the top of ecclesiastical hierarchies.

In addition, atheist propaganda has taken its toll. Millions of Russians have only the vaguest notion of what Christianity teaches. They have been brought up on a steady diet of "religion is superstition" and "science and religion are irreconcilable."

There is a need and a desire for Western Christian help in sharing the gospel. But it is help which ought to recognize, indeed emphasize, the indigenous religious cultures that have been so decimated by the failed Communist experiment. Protestants and Catholics ought not to be shy about how their theological understandings differ from the Orthodox, but they ought to know and appreciate the unique strengths of Orthodoxy. The Orthodox ought to revive and emphasize the jewels of their history and culture, but they ought not to consider Protestants and Catholics as "sheep stealers" among their flocks.

Ignorance of the gospel is so widespread, and the need to rescue people from the tragic dead ends of a spiritual wasteland is so acute, that the different Christian communions dare not squander their energies in quarreling with each other. Compared to the emptiness and meaninglessness of a secular orientation, genuine Christians of all major communions share many essential beliefs. We ought to focus on what we have in common, without denying that there are sometimes significant matters about which we disagree.

The Slavic heartland of the USSR has strong Christian roots, and yet there is a strain of anti-Semitism which must be acknowledged and rejected. Christians ought to insist on freedom of conscience for people of all faiths or no faith.

There are many competitors for the hearts and minds of people in the Soviet Union. Disillusioned atheists may be willing to consider seriously Christian perspectives, but they are also being exposed to other religious perspectives: Buddhist, Mormon, Hare Krishna, and New Age. The siren call of Western consumerism and sensualism is also a powerful contender for attention. Many young people are more interested in a Porsche and provocative Western rock videos than they are a religious renaissance of Russian culture.

There is complete uncertainty as to which way the Soviet Union will go. Though it is unlikely that there will be a revival of Marxist communism or a return to totalitarianism, it is possible that a new Russian-dominated state may emerge which is authoritarian and dictatorial. It is possible that the Baltics, parts of the Caucasus, and eventually the five Central Asian Muslim republics may one day gain their independence, though at present the union authorities are strenuously resisting such a prospect. The outcome in the struggle between the progressive democratic forces and those who resist dismantling the centralized organs of repressive power is very much in doubt. Whether there will be a smooth, or any, transition from a command-communist economy to a free enterprise system is also unknown.

Nor are the signs all positive when it comes to the freedom of the church. Approximately fifteen Christian activists have been murdered or have died in suspicious accidents since 1986—ten of them between April 1990 and February 1991. While churches in general have much more freedom, the KGB still seems to be eliminating some Christian political activists, and occasionally some whose sole crime is the possession of remarkably winsome and attractive spiritual leadership qualities. Just one example: the brutal slaying of Father Alexander Men in September 1990 deprived the Russian Orthodox church of one of its most effective and visionary leaders.

But despite the individual acts of violence and the near certainty of continuing political unrest and economic hardship, there is a strong probability that the recently gained new opportunities for the church will remain substantially in place. There may be some brief flashbacks to the past, but the opportunities for evangelism and growth are likely to persist and even expand.

Western Christians ought to expend much greater efforts and resources than they do at present in exporting religious literature and giving local churches in the USSR the means of printing their own materials. We ought to work as closely as possible with Christians and churches in the Soviet Union to learn from them what they most need and want. We ought to model tolerance and respect for people of other denominational, religious, or nonreligious perspectives. We ought to engage actively in contacts and exchanges of all sorts: academic, professional, and personal. The gospel is frequently most effectively communicated in actions, not words. We ought to encourage some of our most gifted and disciplined young people to commit themselves to serious language training and graduate studies as a means to prepare for long-term missions work. At the present, there are not nearly enough well-qualified Christian personnel to respond to the remarkable opportunities which have developed during recent months.

Turbulent Times for the Soviet Church is a popular, condensed version of *The Soviet Union on the Brink*, which is being released simultaneously. The latter is a completely revised and expanded second edition of my 1989 book, *The Puzzle of the Soviet Church*. At the back of the present work, you will find a brief account of sources used, but for a fully footnoted, indexed, and detailed account of the topics discussed, you should refer to *The Soviet Union on the Brink*. Readers interested in the Siberian Seven emigration case (1978-83)—my entry point to the study of the conditions of the Soviet church—should see the first three chapters of *The Puzzle* or the first chapter of *On the Brink*.

It is not possible in this brief introduction to acknowledge all who have played some part in making this book possible. I am extremely grateful to the Institute on Religion and Democracy (IRD) and its fine staff for supporting me during the research and writing of this book, and to the Lynde and Harry Bradley Foundation for its generous support of the religious liberty programs of the IRD. Special thanks are also due to Michael Bourdeaux, Bohdan R. Bociurkiw, Dmitry Pospielovsky, Theofanis Stavrou, Mark Elliott, and Anita Deyneka. I also wish to thank Robert C. Woodward and Marian Washburn who sparked my interest in Russian culture at Northwest Nazarene College. Special thanks are also due to my graduate school mentor at the University of Washington, Donald W. Treadgold, who many years ago modeled for me the meaning and importance of Christians striving for academic excellence. I wish to acknowledge in gratitude the vision and commitment of Multnomah Press to this book. Without the enthusiastic assistance and encouragement of John Van Diest, Al Janssen, and Rod Morris, this book would not have been possible. Finally, a special thanks to my children Jennifer and Jonathan and my wife Janice for their love and support.

PART I

LEARNING FROM
THE PAST

CHAPTER 1

MARXISM AND CHRISTIANITY:
THE HISTORIC TENSION

*K*arl Marx was obsessed by a vision of humanity freed from the evils of exploitation. Yet in this century some of history's greatest crimes against humanity have been committed in his name. By far more people have perished in the Gulag (network of labor camps) of the Soviet Union, the artificially-induced famines of Ukraine, the "worker's paradise" of Communist China, and the "killing fields" of Cambodia than have died in all the concentration camps of Adolph Hitler. All of these victims have been sacrificed on the altar of the "future happiness of mankind."

The suffering and death inflicted by totalitarian regimes on their own citizens exceeds all the victims of this century's wars. Hitler exterminated some eleven million people in concentration camps; between twenty million and sixty-five million Soviet citizens perished because of Joseph Stalin. This does not include the Soviet Union's staggering World War II losses (perhaps as high as twenty million).

What does all of this have to do with Karl Marx? Surely this is not what he intended. Nor do I think that Vladimir Lenin foresaw the millions who would perish in the Soviet Union at the hands of its own rulers during the quarter century following his death.

THE KEY TO KARL MARX'S LEGACY

There is no more insidious nonsense than that which surrounds discussion of motives. So long as we intend "good" and are fighting "evil," then we are somehow immune from the hard and painful work of examining the consequences of our ideas and our actions. There is no surer recipe for disaster than this illogical and insensitive mind-set. Compassion devoid of disciplined thought is a lethal weapon.

But we are just as inclined to another serious error: the temptation to succumb to "demonization." "Karl Marx was evil." "Lenin was evil." "Communists are evil." The problem is far more complex than these simple judgments reflect. Karl Marx had neither horns nor tail.

When I taught the history of communism at Seattle Pacific University, I frequently startled my classes by having a Marxist come in to make the initial presentation of what Marxists believe. Like Marx, my apologist for Marxism did not have horns, though he did have a beard. The gentleman was a friend of mine and a former professor. He was soft-spoken, answered questions carefully, and threw not a single grenade during the entire two-hour session. He invariably condemned much that had been done in Marx's name, particularly under Stalin. But he also asserted the essential positions of classical Marxism: materialism; atheism; a basically positive view of human nature; and an anti-capitalist, pro-socialist economic analysis.

My students, usually Christians, were surprised to hear someone actually assert and defend non-Christian beliefs about life. Somehow it had seemed less real when their professor contended that such views were held. The students were also pleasantly surprised by the warmth and approachability of the Marxist visitor.

Had Karl Marx made a surprise visit to our class, I think the reaction would have been much the same. He would have appeared more of an academic than a revolutionary. Most of what he wrote, after all, is not easy reading, and is hardly suitable for propaganda. True, Marx was obsessed with his cause, sometimes to the point of sacrificing his family, which he loved. But many Christian pastors have done the same thing, believing that kingdom work was more important than family responsibilities.

Many mistakenly believe that Marx was simply a boring academician, an economist lost in analysis and not accessible to the average person. If this were true, Marxism would never have fired the imaginations of so many revolutionaries. *The Communist Manifesto* (1848) is not an economic primer, but a moving plea for justice. Marx may have been wrong about many things, including the nature of man and ultimate reality, but certain key texts contain sufficient power to move the heart.

Nor is it helpful or accurate to see Marx as some sort of alien Communist striking at the soul of Western man—the originator of the conflict between East and West. Karl Marx is the West. He was German and a full-fledged product of one major stream of Western thought.

Like the typical Enlightenment figure, Karl Marx had great faith in the power of reason and the perfectibility of human beings. He tended to locate evil in human institutions and particular economic arrangements rather than in the hearts and wills of human beings themselves. Though he was dismissive and scathing of the Socialist (particularly Christian) utopians of his day, many of Marx's own expectations for a rosy post-capitalist world were highly utopian. In this too he was unquestionably a child of nineteenth-century Western Europe, where hopes for the future knew almost no bounds.

Marx's ideas are thoroughly Western. From the same secular roots which produced Marxism, other secular fruit has grown: an excessive individualism in some cases, lethargic cynicism and fatalism in others, and frequently ethical relativism disguised as liberal pluralism. Not that these are the only options for secular humanists, but secular philosophies which rule out transcendent realities frequently fall prey to diverse and dangerous pitfalls. This is fully consistent with what orthodox Christianity has always insisted are the natural consequences of failing to come into proper relationship with the Creator.

The lesson for Western Christians is that, however dangerous Marxism in power has been and can be, the same secular forces in somewhat different guises are capable of rotting the foundations of non-Marxist societies. We can collapse entirely by our own devices, or simply so dissipate our strength and character that we are unable or unwilling to resist an outside aggressor.

Marxism in the form of communism in practice has been a modern-day scourge. But many (though not all) of its roots are found in our own backyard.

KARL MARX ON RELIGION

Intense study of the writings and mystique of Karl Marx reveals that atheism was one of the key components of his thought. There was no place in the young Marx's thought for a transcendent God with any claim of sovereignty over human beings.

Sergei Bulgakov, an early Russian Marxist who later converted to Christianity and became a Russian Orthodox priest, wrote a brilliant book on Marx in 1906. In it he argues convincingly that a major source of Marx's entire doctrine was his "militant atheism." Alexander Solzhenitsyn echoed Bulgakov's central thesis in his 1973 letter to Soviet leaders: "Ferocious hostility to religion is Marxism's most persistent feature."

Karl Marx made a virtual declaration of war against any notions of divine transcendence. Religion only exists because human beings seek compensation for what they lack materially. The illusion of religion must be fought because it prevents human beings from seeing the true source of their unhappiness. If those material needs were met, then religion would simply disappear.

ARE MARXISM AND CHRISTIANITY RECONCILABLE?

In their core beliefs, Marxism and Christianity are irreconcilable. To some, such a statement indicates a kind of knee-jerk intolerance, an absence of ecumenism, and a hostility to pluralism. It is none of the above. It is a straightforward, sober judgment based on an analysis of the respective classical positions of each.

It is not a question of ideology, it is a question of logic. If one system believes in God and the other considers belief in a transcendent being wishful thinking, then there is a disagreement. If one system asserts that human beings are inclined to evil and in need of God's divine help, while the other system holds that human beings are basically good and capable of moving towards perfection in their own strength, then there is a basic disagreement. If one system views human beings as a complex mix of spiritual and material components, while the other sees only material and economic factors at work, then again you have a fundamental disagreement.

Given the fundamental differences which divide the two world views, if there sometimes appears to be a synthesis it is invariably because one side or the other has abandoned certain tenets of its own core beliefs. A number of years back, the Mexican liberation theologian José Miranda wrote a book with the subtitle: *The Christian Humanism of Karl Marx*. It should have come as no surprise that Miranda contended that Marx's atheism ought really not concern us that much since there was so much in the German philosopher that was "Christian."

To suggest that Marx is really Christian because he shares with

Christians a concern for humanity is like saying a scientist is really an infant because, like an infant, he needs to sleep and eat. There is an *Alice in Wonderland* flavor to the terms used here which, in the end, makes meaningful dialogue impossible.

For the Christian, to depart from fidelity to the central tenets of the faith is heresy at best, and very likely apostasy. It is the same for the orthodox Marxist. A Marxist who says he now believes in God but remains a Marxist is talking nonsense.

David McLellan, a non-Marxist, pays Karl Marx the ultimate intellectual compliment: he takes him seriously and at his word. "Marxism is a Christian heresy: it has *chosen* part of the Christian gospel relating to this worldly betterment of the human condition, but it has rejected the transcendental dimension. To ask Marxism to become theistic would be to rob it of its specificity."

Sadly, there is frequently a euphoria in certain Christian circles over the possibility of a "new synthesis" emerging from dialogue with Marxists. The danger is that the "new synthesis" will be a product of Christians shedding their former convictions rather than Marxists abandoning theirs. The result can be a political radicalism with a religious veneer. It would be more honest to dispense with the veneer.

Whatever may be the present state of Western theoretical discussions about the relationship between religion and Marxism, in the Soviet Union Karl Marx's views on religion have played a key role in determining the relationship between Christians and the often militantly atheistic state.

THE VARIETIES OF THE MARXIST ATTACK ON RELIGION

One of the most serious errors in Western analysis of the impact of Marxism on religion is the assumption that Marxism always means an all-out attempt to destroy religion. The situation is far more complex, and the threat to religion frequently far more subtle.

We conjure up in our minds perhaps the worst days of the Stalin period, or Albania where all religion was still outlawed as late as April 1991, and visualize all-out war on believers. In fact, attempts to annihilate religion have been relatively rare in the history of Marxism.

More typically, Marxist governments have had to settle for seeking to control or co-opt the churches rather than liquidate them. This less obviously hostile approach is more the product of pragmatism than good will. Religion has been far too strong historically in Marxist countries for there to be any reasonable chance of wiping it out entirely, at least in the short run. It's true that atheist propaganda in virtually all Marxist states predicts that an inevitable scientific and political enlightenment of the people will result in the gradual disappearance of religion. But rushing the day along by direct physical attacks on the churches often has not been considered prudent or possible.

Historically and across the globe, Marxism has dealt with religion in a variety of ways: from attempts to destroy it completely, to efforts to restrict, to a strategy of co-opting churches into the service of the state. Attempts to domesticate and control religion, though not as obviously hostile, represent one of the most insidious forms of government oppression.

As we consider the state of religious freedom in the Soviet Union, we must not forget that Marxism is capable of backing off its outward offensive against religion without abandoning its intention of controlling or manipulating it. It is possible that improvements in the situation of religious believers in the Soviet Union, or elsewhere in the world, may represent a genuine change of heart on the part of the Marxists. It is also possible that control of the church is simply more subtle and less obvious than in the past.

It is imperative that neither alternative be ruled out in advance. Nor can the question be fully addressed without examining in some detail the unique history of Marxism on Russian soil.

MARXISM IN RUSSIA

A major source of atheism and materialism for many Russian revolutionaries was the radical French Enlightenment. If a new intellectual trend or idea emerged in Europe one year, it was likely to turn up a few months later in Russia, often in a more extreme form. Long before the thought of Karl Marx reached Russia, a soil for it had developed which would both nourish it and Russify it. Part of the Russian openness to Marxism in certain circles sprang from the fact that it was the latest idea to come from the "enlightened" political radicals of the West. And part of Russia's receptivity was due to a frustration with the forms of socialism (often utopian and peasant-oriented) which had failed to make much impact in Russia during the 1860s and 1870s.

A common myth of our day is that the Bolshevik Revolution of 1917, which brought proponents of Marxist communism to power, became virtually inevitable from the late nineteenth century on.

Nothing could be further from the truth. In fact, there was an intense debate among the Russian intelligentsia in the early part of the twentieth century over the materialism and atheism which had come to characterize much of the revolutionary movement. One of the high points of the cultural and religious renaissance which followed was the publication in 1909 of Signposts—a collection of essays, mainly by former Marxists, denouncing the dangerous secular elements in the revolutionary movement. Berdyaev, one of these former Marxists, insisted that their commitment to political liberation was no less strong than in the past, but "political liberation is possible only in conjunction with, and on the basis of, a spiritual and cultural renaissance."

Not only did many of the finest intellectuals abandon Marxism, but Russian Marxism itself was riddled by internal divisions. In 1903, the (Marxist) Social Democratic Party split into two factions: Bolshevik and Menshevik. Lenin's faction, the Bolsheviks, insisted on a much smaller and more elite Party membership and pushed for an accelerated and pro-active involvement in bringing about the Revolution.

While the intelligentsia argued over the nature and course of the revolutionary events, there was slow and steady progress in Russia toward a constitutional monarchy. Serfdom, the Russian equivalent of slavery, had been abolished in the 1860s. A whole series of reforms was unleashed over the next few years which pushed Russia in a direction similar to that of its political neighbors in Western Europe. But the tremendous pressures of World War I and the single-minded resolve of Vladimir Lenin were the key factors which led to the eventual victory of the Bolsheviks. Now, for the first time in world history, there would be an attempt to put Marxist ideas into practice.

LENIN AND RELIGION

Though Ilia Ulianov was a devout Orthodox, his son, Vladimir Lenin, broke with religion at age sixteen. This was before he became fully immersed in Marxism. Radical Russian nineteenth-century materialists, such as Dmitry Pisarev and Nicholas Chernyshevsky, had a major early impact on Lenin.

It was as much anti-clericalism as philosophical atheism which shaped Lenin's early critique of religion. He despised Orthodoxy for its intimate connections with the tsarist autocracy which he was committed to destroying. Marx's view that the ruling classes always manipulated the church to maintain their own authority was particularly appealing to Lenin, and the materialism and atheism implicit in the German philosopher's thought was consistent with views Lenin had already picked up in less developed forms from Russian radicals. By 1905, Lenin's views on religion echoed those of Karl Marx:

> Religion is one of the forms of spiritual oppression, which everywhere weighs heavily upon the popular masses, crushed by their perpetual work for others, by want and loneliness. The impotence of the exploited classes in their struggle with the exploiters inevitably gives rise to the belief in a better hereafter, just as the impotence of the savage in his battle with nature gives rise to the belief in gods, devils, miracles, and the like.

In a 1913 letter to Maxim Gorky, Lenin's hatred of the very notion of God reached a new peak of intensity. He declares that the idea of God is "filth, prejudices, sanctification of ignorance and stupor on the one hand, and of serfdom and monarchy on the other."

At first glance, it might seem that a Marxist-Christian dialogue session would last no longer with Lenin than with Marx. However, a more complete examination of his comments reveals that Lenin was capable of taking a moderate tact with religious believers. He particularly disliked "progressive" or moral priests (such clergy did not stir up the people against the church), but in the pre-October Revolution period he did allow priests to work with his revolutionary party, so long as they refrained from religious propaganda.

Lenin could make occasional pronouncements favoring religious freedom. In 1903, for example, he wrote something which can easily be quoted in the age of *glasnost*:

> Everyone should have full freedom not only to adhere to the faith of his choice, *but also to propagate any creed and change his confession.* . . . There should be no "ruling" confession or church. All creeds, all churches should be equal before the law. The priests of different creeds may be maintained by those belonging to the given creed, and the state must not use public funds to support any confession and should not provide maintenance for any clergymen, either Orthodox or Old Believer, sectarian or any other.

This tsarist-era statement was intended to strike a blow at the alliance between the tsarist regime and the Orthodox church, and arguing freedom of religion (particularly for non-Orthodox groups) and championing church/state separation could help weaken the established powers. Once in power, Lenin did proclaim church/state separation, but it was never anything but a cruel hoax. It was Lenin, after all, who deprived the church of the rights of "juridical person," stripped it of the right to own any property, ordered that already published religious literature be withdrawn from sale, and issued an administrative order forbidding the organizing of private religious instruction of young people under the age of eighteen.

How was it possible for Lenin to affirm complete religious freedom and then act in a radically contrary manner? Part of the answer is supplied by Lenin himself in a 1921 memorandum to his foreign affairs commissar, Georgy Chicherin. Dismissing the naive "cultivated circles of Western Europe and America" as "deaf-mutes," he advises his foreign minister to:

> Express our hope to establish immediate diplomatic relations with all capitalist countries on the basis of total non-interference in their internal affairs. The deaf-mutes will believe us. . . . They will even be delighted and will throw their doors wide open. Through these doors will enter the emissaries of the Comintern and our secret service under the cover of diplomatic, cultural, and trade representatives.

To be sure, not just Communist countries have engaged in deception, but there is a deliberate abandonment of ethical norms with Lenin which is frightening. As he declared to Chicherin, "Telling the truth is a bourgeois prejudice. Deception, on the other hand, is often justified by the goal." "We have a new ethics," asserted Lenin's colleague Grigory Zinoviev. "We are permitted to do anything because we are the first in the world to lift the sword, not for the sake of enslavement and oppression, but in the name of universal liberation from slavery." And, of course, one of the things Lenin and Zinoviev sought to liberate humanity from was the prison of religion.

It is a mistake to ignore or minimize what Lenin wrote to the Party faithful regarding religion and ethics. This is critical information, useful in interpreting historical events that follow. One measure of *glasnost* will have to be whether or not specific antireligious views of Marx and Lenin are categorically and publicly rejected. If rejected, will these rejections find their way into the textbooks for their children? And will the future actions of the state be consistent with the publicly announced change of heart?

During Lenin's brief rule until his death in 1924, there was little opportunity to plan the final demise of religion. The main focus had to be on defeating the counter-revolutionary Whites during the Civil War (1917-21) and hanging on to power during an incredibly destructive and anarchic period. Though there was considerable terror used by the Chekha (an early version of the KGB), it was simply not possible to force on the country the collectivism and complete communism which dedicated Marxists wanted.

Lenin even found it necessary, beginning in 1921, to allow a limited return to capitalism (the New Economic Policy) in order to help the economy recover from the devastation caused by the Civil War and early crude attempts to institute radical communism. In the Communist dialectical understanding of the historical moment, this was the "one step back" in the overall pragmatic strategy of "two steps forward, one step back."

The church suffered under Lenin, particularly the Russian Orthodox church; but the worst days of persecution lay ahead, during the reign of Joseph Stalin.

STALIN AND RELIGION

The most important factor in Stalin's relationship to religion was not what he said, but what he did. To be sure, he affirmed the antireligious stances of Marx and Lenin. But more importantly, for a decade and a half he utilized every instrument of state power and terror at his disposal in a concerted effort to liquidate religion. Only during World War II, when he found it necessary to mobilize the moral authority which the church still had among the populace, did he back off an annihilation policy and settle for strict control.

What was new about the Stalin era (1924-1953) was the inauguration of totalitarianism in 1928. This was such a dramatic turning point in Soviet history that it could be labeled a "third revolution." (The first was in February 1917 when the tsarist regime abdicated and was replaced by the basically liberal Provisional government; the second was the Bolshevik Marxist coup of October 1917.) Stalin was not a great thinker, but he was a brilliant tactician. He outmaneuvered better known figures (such as Trotsky, Zinoviev, and Kamenev) through a masterful manipulation of Party appointments. He stands as a constant example of what can be achieved by the person who, for many years, is willing to exercise patience and discipline doing jobs that attract little attention and nobody wants.

By 1928 Stalin had consolidated his power base and was in a position to act. He ruthlessly eliminated virtually all opposition or potential opposition during the next decade. Against the will of the peasant masses he brutally collectivized agriculture. In his quest for dramatic industrial growth, he allocated every available resource for heavy industry. There was virtually no consumer side of the economy. Millions perished during the Stalin era. The churches, its clergy, and its members all experienced tremendous suffering. Some of the most virulent antireligious propaganda was penned during the Stalin era.

Religion has always been a target of totalitarian rulers. The reason is simple. A totalitarian dictator demands a citizen's absolute loyalty. Religion affirms a transcendent focus for human loyalty. Faithful believers of any religion are a constant and stubborn reminder to the totalitarian ruler that he does not enjoy absolute sovereignty. Since believers do not consider death the last reality, even the ultimate power of the state, the power to take a citizen's life, may fail to compel obedience.

THE POST-STALIN ERA AND ATHEISM

Though there was a partial and temporary *glasnost* (they called it a "thaw" in the 1950s) under Nikita Khrushchev (1953-64), the strongly antireligious Marxist views of the past were maintained. The period from 1959 to 1964 was one of particularly vicious persecution of the church. So many churches were closed that even today under Mr. Gorbachev the number of churches open is less than in 1953 when Stalin died.

In an interview with *Pravda* in late 1957, Khrushchev repeated the party line on religion. He insisted that religion was indeed dying out:

> The number of people who believe in God is growing less and less; the youth are growing up, and the overwhelming majority do not believe in God. The enlightenment of the people, the spread of scientific knowledge, the study of the laws of nature leave no room for belief in God.

What he did not say was that he was about to embark on a violent campaign against the churches, evidently not believing his own words about the impending natural death of religion.

There has been a consistent attitude toward religion in the Kremlin from the time of Lenin right up to the 1980s. The arrival of Brezhnev on the scene in the 1960s was accompanied by a stupefying recital of the cardinal principles of Marxist-Leninism: "We should remember Lenin's words, that in our society everything which serves to build up communism is moral." But it was under Brezhnev that the failure of Soviet Marxism to provide either liberty or prosperity for its people became particularly obvious.

There have been some remarkable shifts in official attitudes toward religion in the Soviet Union in recent years. But even well into the Gorbachev era, the admonition to the Party faithful stressed that they remain resolute in pursuing a vigorous atheist policy. Mr. Gorbachev himself, in a November 26, 1986 speech in Soviet Central Asia (Tashkent), called for "a decisive and uncompromising struggle against manifestations of religion and strengthening of political work with the masses and of atheist propaganda."

Conclusion

Why the persistent theme of atheism in classical and Soviet Marxism? Why the compulsion to attack religion, rather than simply be amused by those who childishly believe in illusions? After all, many would argue that what is best in Marxism is its passionate attack on injustice. Laying aside for a moment the appalling record of what Marxism has produced, the theory at least sounds laudable: end injustice, bring equality, and provide for the basic needs of the masses. So why all the fuss about atheism?

This is the critical issue. *Marxism is not simply socialism which happens to be atheist; it is atheism which happens to be socialist.* Christian socialism which is not compulsory may or may not work economically, but it does not represent a challenge to the faith. In contrast, atheistic Marxism strikes at the very heart of religion because it places man, rather than God, at the center of the universe.

The humanitarian quest sometimes is but a cloak for a fundamental rejection of God and his valuing of freedom. We make the world over in our own image, and that means a repudiation of the world created according to God's will. The issue is not whether it is appropriate to care for the poor. The issue is whether we have the right to deprive them of their freedom in order to force on them a particular secular definition of "the good."

The Marxism of Karl Marx and his followers in the Soviet Union is intimately associated with an uncompromising stance on atheism. Nor is this just atheism in the abstract, but an active struggle against religion as a threat to the claims of totalitarian power.

The implications of this are sobering. Improvements for believers in the Gorbachev era can be real and encouraging. Yet they may not touch the core issues which have traditionally driven classical or Russian Marxism's profound hostility to religion. Apart from a fundamental departure from and rejection of central tenets or interpretations of Marxism, true religious freedom in the Soviet Union can never be more than an illusion.

In the providence of God, genuine change involving fundamental religious freedom is possible in the Soviet Union. But we do not hasten its coming by minimizing how radical the departure will have to be from past theory and practice.

CHAPTER 2

CHURCH AND STATE IN THE SOVIET UNION: 1917 TO 1985

I. REVOLUTION TO WORLD WAR II

*I*t is estimated that during the first six years of Soviet rule, when Vladimir Lenin was still at the helm of state, twenty-eight Russian Orthodox bishops and more than twelve hundred priests perished at the hands of the Bolsheviks. During the decades which followed, most of the fifty-four thousand Russian Orthodox churches which existed in 1914 were destroyed, shut down, or turned into warehouses, factories, or other "socially-useful" enterprises. Of Stalin's millions of victims, many died specifically because of their religious convictions. Many other Christians were swallowed up by the indiscriminate terror and inhumane economic policies of the Stalin years.

A Tale of People, Not Numbers

The problem with statistics is that they numb the brain without touching the heart. It is hard to feel any sympathy with nameless numbers; but it is almost impossible not to be moved by the story of any one of the anonymous figures who make up the cold totals.

Consider Father Pavel. Before the Revolution, Father Pavel was a typical priest in charge of a busy parish in what was then called St. Petersburg (Leningrad). His wife was swept into the whirlwind of the Revolution and became an atheist lecturer, though she remained married. With each passing day of the new regime, life got tougher for Father Pavel.

Finally, the awful moment came. Like many others, Father Pavel found himself in prison, then in exile. But it was during his confinement that the most remarkable period of his ministry began. Though he lived but three short years after his arrest, and despite being confined to his cell and then to his sickbed in exile, he managed to inspire and help virtually all who came in contact with him. Hardened criminals became believers through his steadfast faith. On the evening he died, half the collective farm turned out to pay their respects.

Behind every number mentioned and church counted are tales like that of Father Pavel. Behind the statistics we find suffering, persecution, physical deprivation, separated families, and bereaved children. And we find those moments of truth when an individual must stand alone and make decisions of faith which will dramatically affect one's career, one's family, even one's very life. But most of all, the story behind the facts is one of hope and resilience—the victory of faith over cynicism, the triumph of those who believe in the one true God over those who have put their faith in false gods. Tertullian, the third-century theologian, was right when he reflected on two centuries of Roman persecution of the Christians: "The more you mow us down, the more we grow; the seed is the blood of Christians."

CHURCH AND STATE IN RUSSIA BEFORE THE REVOLUTION

Religion in the Soviet Union cannot be understood apart from an awareness of two things about pre-revolutionary Russia. First, Russian culture is profoundly religious. Russian literature, architecture, music, and art are permeated with a sense of the importance of God, faith, and religious tradition. Even the religious skeptic, secular revolutionary, and cynic existed within a framework which would have been incomprehensible apart from a knowledge of religious language and symbols.

Second, the relationship between the Russian Orthodox church and the tsarist government during the two centuries prior to the Bolshevik Revolution had an important impact on the relationship which developed between the Communist rulers and the Russian Orthodox hierarchy. Peter the Great, tsar of Russia from 1689 to 1725, was the great Westernizer. He was also the tsar who virtually transformed the Russian Orthodox church into a department of government.

The close ties between the Russian Orthodox church and the

tsarist regime put the church in a vulnerable position when the revolution came. Revolutionaries viewed the church as a prop of the old regime that would need to be destroyed.

The subservience of the church to the tsarist government not only put it in danger with the new government, but provided a historical precedent for the Communists not allowing the church to exist independent from the state. Of course, there was one major difference. The new leaders were dogmatically and vocally opposed to the very idea of religion. Ultimately, they wanted to see religion disappear as a factor in national and social life.

Despite the subservient position of the Russian Orthodox church under both tsars and commissars, it was immeasurably worse off under the new regime. It is regrettable if the church is compelled in any sense to be a handmaiden for the politics of the state. But it is a much more fundamental indignity to not even be allowed the freedom to practice one's faith. This is precisely what was imposed on the Russian Orthodox church under the Communist rulers.

The church in the hands of the Soviet authorities was much like a mouse in the paws of a cat; there was little question what the cat ultimately intended to do with the mouse.

THE RUSSIAN ORTHODOX CHURCH: 1917-1923

Initially, however, the cat was in no position to destroy the mouse within its grasp. Its own survival was too much at stake to have the luxury of making careful plans for the liquidation of the church. That the Russian Orthodox church had to be crippled, however, was obvious to Lenin and his comrades.

One of the first major blows against the church came with the November 1917 decree which nationalized all land. The church had huge holdings which were affected by this decision. The fate of religious communities was directly in the hands of the new secular authorities. In the early period of the Revolution, the government confiscated six thousand churches and monastic buildings because they had historical or archaeological value to the state. In January 1918, a decree seized for the state all bank account holdings of all religious associations.

A government decree in June 1921 forbade any sermons that were not purely religious in subject matter. Other direct actions against the church came in the spring of 1923. The closure of churches was legalized when the buildings were deemed useful to the state. Furthermore, a religious association could be dissolved on the basis of "political unreliability and anti-Sovietism."

Another tactic was to allow a local church to be used for religious purposes certain days of the week, but to allow dances and clubs to function in the church on the other days. When church members refused to hold services in the building because they considered it desecrated by this secular use, the church was officially closed down. The government excuse was that such closures were according to the wishes of the parishioners.

By 1920, 673 out of 1,025 monasteries which had existed in 1914 had been dissolved by the authorities. But one of the most vicious and dishonest moves against the church was yet to occur—the confiscation of all church resources under the cover of raising funds for starving citizens.

A terrible famine caused by droughts and the economic side effects of Civil War descended on the Soviet Union in the summer of 1921 and lasted a full year. The Orthodox church immediately stepped in to help. Patriarch Tikhon launched a campaign to raise funds from every community within the church to feed those with nothing to eat. But the ecclesiastical relief committee was ordered dissolved by the government, and all that it had collected was given to the state Famine Relief Committee. This is the first known example of Communist Russian rulers virtually outlawing independent church charity work.

One might think the primary reason for the government's attack on independent famine relief was that the church would be positively perceived by society. Actually, the main reason was the desire to strip the church of its material possessions, and the famine provided the cover for these massive expropriations.

It was hard, however, for the government to find a publicly defensible way to carry out the attack on the church's resources; after all, the church was being extremely generous. In February 1922, the patriarch called on the parochial councils to donate all church items of value, except those used in administering the Sacraments. Nine days later, the government ordered all church valuables handed over to the Famine Relief Committee. The patriarch responded in a pastoral letter that sacramental valuables could not be surrendered.

Finally, the government had its long-awaited excuse. "The church was selfishly refusing to help the starving!" A campaign of terror and forced confiscation of valuables was launched throughout the country. The Soviet press itself reported fourteen hundred incidents involving bloodshed as a result of the campaign to confiscate church possessions.

In Petrograd (soon to be renamed Leningrad) Metropolitan Veniamin worked out a conciliatory way to avoid unnecessary bloodshed and confrontation. Believers were to be allowed to contribute from their own private resources amounts equivalent to the value of the sacramental items. At first it appeared this compromise was going to work, but finally the hardline opponents of the popular metropolitan prevailed. Veniamin and three others were executed in 1922. In all, between 1921 and 1923, twenty-seven hundred married priests, thirty-four hundred nuns, and many laymen were killed in the government's confiscation of church valuables for "famine relief."

THE SHACKLES OF REGISTRATION

As early as 1922, Soviet rulers required religious societies to register with the local government. Thus, many years before the notorious 1929 religious sect laws, the pattern was established for using registration as a way of controlling and intimidating believers. Local authorities could set up all sorts of special criteria for registering, which, if accepted, would effectively harness a church's activities. If a church refused to register under those conditions, the magistrates would have a pretext for taking action against it.

Patriarch Tikhon's case illustrates the terrible dilemmas of that period. He showed both courage and accommodation as he tried to keep the Orthodox church unified during difficult days. In February 1925, Tikhon applied for registration with the state authorities. Before the authorities responded, the patriarch died suddenly, probably at the hands of the secret police. Metropolitan Peter became the acting head of the church. He was informed that the conditions for registration included making statements the authorities required, excluding from official positions those bishops the government did not approve, and working with the government person in charge of religious affairs, who worked for the secret police.

Metropolitan Peter refused to register under these conditions, and by the end of 1925 he was imprisoned. Peter's replacement, Sergy, felt he had no choice but to seek registration, which he did in June 1926. It was Sergy's intention to bend but not break. He asserted in a letter to his clergy that the church ought not to be involved in politics nor ought it "enter into any special involvement" to prove its loyalty.

Soviet officials were not satisfied with the extent of Sergy's capitulation, and in December 1926 he too was arrested along with 117 bishops. This mass arrest and the subsequent compromise was an important turning point in Soviet church history. Historian Matthew Spinka asserts that the secret police "succeeded in purging the Church of all who possessed moral courage to oppose the policies of the state. This . . . was the process of 'eradication of the best.' "

Because Soviet authorities managed to place sufficiently docile church hierarchs in leadership positions, the notion has grown up in the West that the Orthodox church has never shown any courage or independence. This is not true. Consider the case of Metropolitan Kiril.

In the spring of 1927, while Sergy was still in jail, authorities tried to convince the man most likely to become the next patriarch, Kiril, to accept the conditions for registration. When one official tried to impress on the churchman the necessity of removing a bishop from his See, if the Soviets demanded it, Kiril responded, "If the bishop is guilty of an ecclesiastic offense, I shall do so. But otherwise I would call him and tell him: 'Brother, I've nothing against you, but the civil authorities want to retire you, and I am forced to do so.' "

But the Communist bureaucrat was not satisfied. "No, you must pretend the initiative is yours, and find some accusation." Metropolitan Kiril would not budge. "You are not a cannon, and I am not a shell with which you want to destroy the Church from within." On the same day this confrontation occurred, Kiril was sent back into Arctic exile, where he died seventeen years later.

Shortly after the refusal to compromise Kiril, the Soviets released Sergy from prison (March 1927). Sergy had been sufficiently broken to say much of what the Communists wanted. His "Declaration of Loyalty" (July 1927) caused a stir in the church world. Sergy asserted that he wanted the Soviet government to understand that it was possible to be both a serious Orthodox Christian and a loyal Soviet citizen. He told the emigre clergy that if they did not pledge their loyalty to the Soviet government, he would take them off the list of patriarchal clergy.

Though Sergy had been forced to compromise, he did not go nearly as far as the Soviets would have liked. Still the July 1927 declaration had, as emigre historian Nikita Struve put it, "transformed the church into an active ally of the Soviet government." The majority of the clergy and their parishioners, however, understood that "this sin was necessary to save the church from destruction."

A Twentieth-Century Classic: The Solovky Memorandum

At the time Metropolitan Sergy was deciding there was no way out for the church short of major compromise, another powerful section of the church was coming to a different conclusion. Two months before Sergy's July declaration, the bishops imprisoned at Solovky issued one of the most profound and moving Christian documents of the entire Soviet era.

Located in the frigid Arctic White Sea, the Solovky (Solovetsky) Islands were one of the initial outposts of the Soviet labor camp system. A monastery was founded on the largest Solovky island in the fifteenth century. From 1718 to 1903 the tsars had used parts of the monastery as a prison, but the monastery itself continued to function until the October Revolution.

The origins of the Gulag archipelago—the phrase Alexander Solzhenitsyn used to describe the system of labor camps sprinkled across the Soviet map—are found on the Solovky Archipelago. The first batch of prisoners was brought here in the early 1920s, while Lenin was still in charge. The monks had already been forced to become collective farmers on the grounds, but now the old men were evicted. Within a few months, the agricultural productivity of the monks was a relic of the past.

An account of the terrors on Solovky Islands, told by one who miraculously managed to escape, was published in England in the late 1920s. Embarrassed by the questions which the account raised, the esteemed Soviet author Maxim Gorky was sent to investigate in 1929. Despite the bravery of a boy who told Gorky the terrible truth about the abuse and murder of prisoners, Gorky came back and reported that the prisoners were well treated. The boy was taken out and shot shortly after Gorky left. On a single awful night in October 1929, exactly three hundred prisoners were executed, almost as many as the total number the tsars had incarcerated there during the centuries it was used as a prison.

However, the Solovky camps produced not just death, but also an immortal statement on church/state relations.

The Solovky memorandum brilliantly combines three separate themes. First, the bishops argue convincingly that the government had seriously undermined its own decree on the separation of church and state. The state is systematically and aggressively intervening in the internal affairs of the church by supporting one minority group (the Renovationists) while persecuting any who will not support it. Further, the state is not allowing the church to provide religious education for its young people and is shutting down monasteries.

Second, the bishops display a keen sense of the philosophical differences between Christianity and Marxist communism. Their sober sense of reality about the differences between Christianity and classical Marxism has been sadly missing in many Western discussions in recent years.

Third, despite the deep philosophical differences, coexistence is possible under certain circumstances. These bishops were not reactionary, "fight to the death" anti-Communists. Their memorandum reminds us that Christians have managed to survive within such diverse political systems as the Ottoman Turkish Empire and democratic America, and they did so by "rendering unto Caesar that which is Caesar's, and unto God, that which is God's."

But coexistence can succeed, according to the bishops, only if there is a separation of church and state. If the Soviets will respect Lenin's own decree on the separation of church and state, coexistence can work. The church is willing not to involve itself in the activities of the government and is willing for its members to discharge their civic duties. But the state must not interfere with the church's internal spiritual affairs.

The bishops acknowledge that during the Civil War immediately following the Bolshevik seizure of power, the church did oppose the political authorities. But this was to be expected, note the bishops, since criminals in the name of, but not necessarily with the authorization of, the new state were arbitrarily acting against the church. That day is past, and order has returned. There is now no need to oppose the government.

The conclusion is straightforward and to the point. If the Soviet government agrees to coexistence based on true separation of church and state, then the church "will rejoice at the justice of those on whom such policies depend." If not, "she is ready to go on suffering, and will respond calmly, remembering that her power is not in the wholeness of her external administration, but in the unity of faith and love of her children; but most of all she lays her hopes upon the unconquerable power of her divine Founder."

That the Solovky memorandum was composed by courageous

Russian Orthodox bishops ought to temper the harsh judgments sometimes launched against the Orthodox church. True, these bishops were barred from leadership in the church, many paying the ultimate price for their courage. But within the Orthodox church there have always been those who challenged the view that timid compromise is required for survival. Even now there is a bitter dispute between the official hierarchy and Orthodox dissidents.

Much of what followed this first decade of Soviet rule is simply a variation on the themes of this earliest period. It is significant that these themes were well established under Lenin and Stalin before the totalitarian period began at the end of the 1920s.

Non-Orthodox Christians in the Russian Empire, particularly native Russians or Ukrainians, experienced much discrimination and persecution during the tsarist period. There were only occasional moments of toleration. For this vibrant Christian minority, the arrival of the Bolsheviks spelled greater freedom than any they had known under the tsars. In time, their lot would become virtually identical to or worse than that of their Orthodox brothers and sisters, but this was not the case during the first decade.

The Evangelical "Golden Age": 1917-1929

The Communist rulers' decision to leave the evangelicals alone was a major miscalculation. The authorities failed not only to understand that the growth of the evangelicals would not necessarily undermine the Orthodox church, they seriously underestimated how much growth would occur.

The Orthodox church itself grew despite the persecution of the 1920s. Even a Soviet source recognized that "at least since 1923 there was felt a rise in religiosity across the whole country." But it was the growth of the evangelicals that forced the Communists to sit up and take notice. The evangelical church grew from 107,000 baptized members in 1905 to 350,000 by 1921 and to 500,000 by 1929. These figures do not even include the Pentecostals, who by 1928 had grown to over 17,000 members.

Pacifism was common among Russian Baptists and evangelical Christians, and at first the new Soviet government accommodated these believers. In 1919 the government permitted exemptions from military service for reasons of conscience, and more than forty thousand were eventually given permission not to serve.

However, by the early 1920s the "Golden Age" had a few clouds.

The Communist authorities became increasingly intolerant toward pacifists, and by the late 1920s, the pacifist exemption became a dead letter. Under the intensifying pressure and the threat of prison, most evangelical groups abandoned or compromised their views on nonviolence over the next several decades.

Between 1929 and 1935, the number of evangelicals declined dramatically (by about 50 percent) providing stark evidence of a sharp change in Soviet policy. The evangelical upsurge had deeply disturbed the Party leaders. Hopes that religion would quietly die out were proving unfounded. "Active" opposition to evangelicals became the order of the day.

An important part of the spread of evangelical ideas was the printing of religious literature and Bibles. But the printing of Bibles ended in 1927, and twenty-nine years would pass before they were printed again on Soviet soil.

THE NIGHTMARE YEARS: 1929-1939

Totalitarianism came to the Soviet Union at the end of the 1920s. Following Lenin's death in 1924, Stalin cleverly eliminated virtually all of his major rivals. He was now ready to force on the country an accelerated industrialization plan aimed at making sure the Soviet Union would catch up with the more advanced West. Furthermore, he intended to collectivize agriculture by force and to terrorize the population into absolute submission to the state. The state was identified entirely with the will of Stalin, who spoke with unquestioned authority for the Communist party. By the time the terror ended, millions were dead.

The realization of a totalitarian vision requires the liquidation of independent or rival sources of authority. Thus, any religious group is in great danger when a ruler begins to act with totalitarian intent.

One of Stalin's first acts of aggression against the church was the April 1929 law dealing with religious cults. The alleged purpose of the law was to provide the rules under which communities of twenty or more could become legally recognized by the state. In fact, according to historian Walter Sawatsky, the law "served as the pretext for closing most of the churches, arresting the ministers, and bringing evangelical church life to a standstill." According to the law: minors could not go to church; special meetings could not be arranged for young people, children, and women; church libraries were not permitted; and individual churches were not even allowed to give material assistance to their own.

The damage done to the church between 1929 and 1943 was staggering. An estimated forty-two thousand priests lost their lives between 1918 and 1940; most of those perished in the 1930s. If a priest was lucky enough to beat the mortality rates in Stalin's prisons (80-90 percent did not come out), he had virtually no chance of ever being a priest again. Massive church closings occurred. By 1933, five hundred of Moscow's six hundred churches had been closed. By 1941, ninety-eight out of every one hundred Orthodox churches were closed down.

Orthodox and Protestant alike now felt the hard boot of the atheist state. Typical is the experience of the Pentecostal leader Ivan Voronaev. After enjoying dramatic growth in the 1920s and even publishing eight issues in 1928 of a Pentecostal periodical called *Evangelist*, his world came crashing down. After midnight on July 6, 1930, Stalin's secret police barged in, searched his house, and took Ivan away. Voronaev was accused of being a spy for imperialist America, and the fact that he had received some financial support from the Assemblies of God and the Russian and East European Mission was used as evidence against him.

In 1933, Ivan's wife, Katherine, followed her husband into the camps of Siberia. Both were in and out of exile and labor camps for the next several years. Ivan perished in the camps, probably during the early 1950s. According to a recent Pentecostal emigre, he was killed by being placed in a cell with vicious dogs. He lies in an unknown Siberian grave. Katherine was freed in 1953, following Stalin's death, and eventually emigrated to the United States.

AT WHAT PRICE SURVIVAL? THE TRAGEDY OF SERGY

The unsavory relationship between the acting patriarch of the Orthodox church, Metropolitan Sergy, and the totalitarian rulers was becoming an even greater cause for bitterness. Though many have had nothing but contempt for Sergy, his plight was more tragic than treacherous. It is true that he deliberately lied to the world about the status of the Russian Orthodox church. He told foreign correspondents in 1930 that there was no persecution of religion in the Soviet Union, and he repeated the assertion in his book *The Truth about Religion in Russia,* published during the war. (The book had little distribution in the USSR; it was intended for foreign consumption.)

But Sergy had convinced himself that the survival of the church depended on such lies. He told a priest who challenged his false statement that the authorities had written the statement for him. In addition, the authorities kept him under arrest for a week while threatening to arrest every remaining bishop and destroy the main church administration if he did not sign the document. Sergy felt he had no choice but to sign.

Sergy was gambling that his capitulation would purchase the survival of the church. As the years passed, however, and the church's survival was more and more in doubt, even Sergy realized that the painful concessions he had made had not pacified Stalin.

We should not be too quick to judge those who have faced choices most of us will never have to make. But we also ought to be aware of the radically different response others have made to the Communist authorities. The Solovky bishops offered coexistence with the authorities, but not at the price of the betrayal of their most fundamental beliefs. Sergy was obsessed with maintaining the skeleton of the church, the administrative structure. But what is that worth if the living flesh of the body—the priests and the people—lose respect for the structure? The Solovky bishops had a different conception of the essence of the church. If the state will not accept honorable coexistence, said the bishops, then the church is ready to go on suffering.

Alexander Solzhenitsyn's advice to all who must deal with those who would shackle and enslave is: *"Never believe them, never fear them, never ask them for anything."* The courageous Russian Orthodox poet Irina Ratushinkaya, released on the eve of the Reagan/Gorbachev summit in October 1986, credits the survival of her spirit in labor camp to following Solzhenitsyn's advice.

II. World War II through Khrushchev

Stalin must bear at least partial responsibility for the twenty million Soviet citizens who died in World War II. Stalin's purges were so sweeping that he wiped out most of his senior officer corps. In addition, he badly misread Hitler's intentions. When Hitler invaded the USSR in 1941, the country was not prepared for the onslaught. As terrible as the war was for the Soviet Union, it did compel Stalin to seek help from the very institution he was trying to liquidate—the church.

THE MERCIES OF WAR: THE CHURCH REVIVES

The big breakthrough for the church occurred on September 4, 1943, when Stalin met with Sergy and three other metropolitans in his Kremlin office. That something was radically different was obvious when Sergy arrived from Ulianovsk the day before the meeting. Instead of being taken to his unpretentious wooden house, a government car took him to the luxurious home of the former German Ambassador.

Stalin had decided to make a shift from a policy of virtual annihilation of the church to that of co-optation. He found he desperately needed the church's help because of the war. As a result of the meeting, which lasted from shortly after 9 P.M. until 3 A.M., Stalin agreed to open many churches and seminaries, and a church council was to be held to elect a patriarch (since one had not been formally elected since Tikhon's death in 1926). Four days later a council of nineteen bishops elected Sergy as patriarch. Although exact information is not available, Stalin may have eventually allowed as many as half the number of pre-revolutionary Orthodox churches to reopen.

The new relationship between church and state was regulated by the Council for Russian Orthodox Church Affairs, created in 1943. In July 1944 a similar body—the Council for the Affairs of Religious Cults—was created to deal with the Protestants. These councils were combined in 1965 to form the Council for Religious Affairs, which continues to exist today.

Just eight months after his historic meeting with Stalin, Sergy died and was replaced by Aleksy, who served as patriarch until his death in 1971.

One final development deserves to be noted. During World War II a policy emerged whereby one person among the senior Orthodox hierarchy was assigned by the Kremlin the task of maintaining the "foreign policy" portfolio of the church. This was the person with whom the authorities maintained closest contact, in whom they had the greatest trust, and who would invariably parrot the Kremlin foreign policy line abroad or with foreign visitors.

During the last years of Sergy's life, Metropolitan Nikolai carried out this function in part. But under Patriarch Aleksy, the division of labor became more pronounced. Not surprisingly, it was Nikolai who became the head of the Department of External Ecclesiastical Relations. An example of how the Soviets intended to use their patriarchal foreign policy contact emerged in late May 1945. Patriarch Aleksy traveled to the Middle East with Nikolai to, according to historian Dmitry Pospielovsky, "impress the noncommunist world that the Russian Church was a genuine and 'free' institution, i.e., that the Soviet state had changed for the better and that all anticommunist propaganda in this respect was grossly exaggerated."

In the fall of 1944, the All-Union Council of Evangelical Christians-Baptists (AUCECB) was formed. Though the results of the unity congress pleased the Evangelical Christians and Baptists who participated, the Soviet state was also certain that it had something to gain. The state, therefore, had provided the transportation to bring the forty-five delegates to the meeting, and then had taken care of all food and housing costs.

Like the Orthodox, the Protestants who cooperated with the authorities felt obliged to do homage to Stalin. The unity congress dutifully sent a telegram to Stalin thanking him for taking care of the needs of Christians.

CHURCH AND STATE: 1945-1959

By 1947 any hopes that the hiatus in state-sponsored antireligious propaganda might continue permanently were dashed. The Communist youth paper *Komsomol Pravda* declared it was impossible to be both a Komsomol member and a believer. The main teacher's newspaper attacked the notion that there could be a nonreligious education, insisting that education had to be vigorously antireligious.

After the war, a more sinister use of the Orthodox church was hatched in the Kremlin. The church would be used in the front lines of a "peace offensive" aimed at the West. Moscow's chief concern was the substantial lead the United States had in military power, especially in nuclear weapons.

Few pages in the history of the church's subservience to the Soviet authorities can compare with the role the Orthodox church played in the peace initiatives. At the first USSR Conference for Peace held in August 1949, Metropolitan Nikolai called the United States "the rabid fornicatress of resurrected Babylon . . . [who] is trying to seduce the people of the world while pushing them toward war." The wartime alliance between the United States and the Soviet

Union was obviously breaking up. Subtlety was not one of Nikolai's virtues as he trumpeted in the name of the Russian Orthodox church the crude propaganda of the puppetmaster.

If only the first impulse that grips us when confronted with apparently black and white judgments were correct. Alas, reality is often more complicated and more tragic. Even Nikolai, the crude propagandist for Stalin, had another side. Russian believers were fond of his moving sermons and considered his propagandist work a necessary evil. In contrast to the 1920s and early 1930s, when parishioners rebuked clerics simply for praying for the Soviet rulers, the parishioners were now silent. As Pospielovsky puts it, "The lie has become an accepted part of life!"

To be sure, many Russian Orthodox faithful disagreed that the lies were justified. To lie and practice religious piety simultaneously requires strenuous mental and spiritual gymnastics, though it is far less rare than we might like to admit. However, it is not easy to maintain a sense of right and wrong in the process.

Strong statements of support for the Communist government were not confined to the Orthodox church. Registered leaders of the All-Union Council of Evangelical Christians-Baptists (AUCECB) cooperated as well. In 1947, Jacob Zhidkov, one of the main leaders of the Baptists, wrote in their official journal, *Fraternal Messenger*: "God not only established but also strengthened the Soviet state. As a result the Soviet land became the chief of all freedom-loving peoples in its unceasing struggle for peace, for social and political justice."

That same year Zhidkov lied about the state of religious freedom in the Soviet Union: "Evangelical Christians-Baptists have full freedom, not only for their divine services but also to conduct the necessary activities embracing all aspects of our religious life."

The evangelicals experienced a revival in the months following the end of World War II, but within a couple of years the horizon clouded with an impending new Stalin crackdown on religion. Stalin's last five years were difficult ones for evangelicals. Between 1948 and 1953 there were almost no contacts with foreigners, and unregistered believers often received twenty-five-year sentences for allegedly violating Article 58 of the criminal code—"anti-soviet" slander.

KHRUSHCHEV'S ASSAULT ON THE CHURCH: 1959-1964

Many are shocked to learn that in the 1960s, well after the Stalin horrors had supposedly passed, a new wave of violent suppression occurred. A decision was made at the highest levels, and the assault on believers in the press and the schools followed soon after. The legal code was changed to make it even easier to incriminate believers. This campaign was well organized and directed from Moscow. The person behind it was Nikita Khrushchev, reputed to be liberal by Soviet standards and the man who had delivered a secret speech at the XX Party Congress in 1956 denouncing some of Stalin's actions.

The attack on the church went well beyond an intensification of atheist propaganda; it included a physically violent campaign against the church and its members. Some children were forcibly taken from their parents because a religious upbringing was allegedly causing them psychological damage.

While church meetings were brutally broken up, Orthodox monasteries were also targeted for violent "administrative" measures. Pilgrims on the way to the Pochaev monastery in Ukraine were attacked en masse by the police. Women in the group were raped. One young woman, who had taken her vows of chastity and often attended services at the monastery, was dragged from her home by the police, raped, then dragged up to her own attic and thrown out the window. She died a few hours later. Several monks were forcibly committed to a mental hospital, and one died two months later. Another monk died during interrogation. His body, returned to his parents, showed signs of severe torture.

In the western Siberian town of Kulunda, Nikolai Khmara, a recent convert from a life of drunkenness, was arrested and sentenced to prison for his activities in an unregistered congregation. Since becoming a Christian, Nikolai had become a fine family man and a strong member of the church. Just two weeks after his trial, his family was informed that he had died in prison. Though they were told not to, the Kulunda Christians opened Nikolai's coffin and discovered his badly mutilated body. His tongue had been torn out, as had his fingernails and toenails; his body was covered with burns. Fellow prisoners later reported that his tormentors had finally ripped out his tongue because he would not stop talking about Christ.

The authorities subjected believers to vicious attacks in the press as well. In one 1960 example of slander, monks were charged with raping female pilgrims, and mass secret abortions were allegedly performed in monasteries to hide the illicit sexual liaisons of the nuns and monks.

The leaders of the Orthodox church showed more courage in dealing with the vigorous assault on religion than did the leaders of AUCECB. Patriarch Aleksy wrote several letters to Khrushchev protesting the persecutions and requesting a personal audience with him. He did not get a response. But what showed particular courage was Aleksy's public pronouncement in February 1960 at a Conference of the Soviet Public for Disarmament. After listing all the wonderful things the church had given to Russia, the patriarch stated:

> Yet, despite all this, Christ's Church, whose very aim is human well-being, is suffering insults and attacks from humans. . . . Jesus Christ himself predicted indestructibility of the Church when he said: "The gates of hell will not overcome the *Church*."

The patriarch's uncharacteristic and unexpected comments unleashed a barrage of verbal attacks. "You want to assure us that the whole Russian culture has been created by the Church . . . this is not true!" shouted a member of the audience.

The great irony is that it was Metropolitan Nikolai, the sycophant to the Kremlin on foreign policy, who had written the patriarch's speech. This is probably the reason Nikolai was forced to retire as head of the church's Department of External Ecclesiastical Relations. Also a factor in his falling out with the Soviet overlords was a collection of his unpublished sermons which responded strongly to atheist attacks on religion. Such is the mystery of life that within the same breast can beat both the heart of a coward and of a man of courage.

By the end of 1960, Patriarch Aleksy had no more energy to resist, and he quietly submitted to what was expected of him. In July 1961 he helped force on the church changes in its statutes which stripped the individual priest of administrative authority over his parish. Local power was now in the hands of an executive committee of three from the parish community. The Soviets had insisted on this, certain that it would make it easier to have their way with the churches. They were right. Fortunately, religious *perestroika* in the Gorbachev era is allowing the restoration of local administrative authority to the individual priest.

SCHISM AMONG THE EVANGELICALS

The conduct of the AUCECB during the Khrushchev era was anything but courageous. The leadership was so timid and capitulatory that a major split occurred within its ranks—a split which survives to this day.

To avoid confrontation with the secular authorities, the AUCECB revised its church statutes to bring them into conformity with the 1929 law on religious cults. In the summer of 1960 the senior Protestant leaders sent these revised statutes and a "Letter of Instruction" to their senior presbyters. The letter does not reflect evangelical convictions. It forbids children to attend church services and makes reference to "unhealthy missionary tendencies." One wonders what had happened to Christ's commandment "to go into all the world and make disciples," for registered AUCECB leaders assert: *"the chief goal of religious services at the present time is not the attraction of new members but satisfaction of the spiritual needs of believers."* Tens of thousands of registered Protestants felt betrayed by their leaders.

During the early 1960s believers found themselves restricted not only by the very limiting 1929 rules but also by secret guidelines never made public. The government councils of religion (there were still two until the end of 1965) that controlled the Orthodox and the Protestants would give church leaders verbal instructions which were often not part of any written, formally-declared government policy. Those who protested were frequently arrested.

AN APPRAISAL OF THE KHRUSHCHEV PERSECUTION

Two factors may help explain why Khrushchev launched his antireligious offensive. First, the post-Stalin Communist leaders' objections to Stalin's tyranny did not include disagreement with his fundamental hostility to religion. These leaders recognized the great dangers in a "cult of personality," not the least being the threat to their own lives. But Stalin's shortcomings did not alter their own fidelity to classical Marxist notions on religion.

Second, Soviet leaders had to face a reality that Karl Marx never did—they had to contend with religious belief which refused to wither away. We don't know what Marx would have done under such circumstances. Would he have revised his views of human nature, given the evidence that there was something to religious consciousness besides unmet economic needs? We don't know, of course. But we do know that Marxist states have often succumbed to the temptation to force the decline of religion when it refuses to disappear on its own.

At the end of the Khrushchev era the upper echelons of the Party conducted an evaluation of the antireligious campaign. "Their general conclusion," according to historian Dmitry Pospielovsky, "was that it had not paid off." The church had survived, though much of it had been driven underground—a situation potentially more dangerous to the regime than if the church were above ground and on a leash.

Soviet self-criticism of past religious practices did not begin with Gorbachev. The Central Committee of the Communist party released a declaration in November 1964 titled "On Errors Committed in the Conduct of Atheist Propaganda." This document followed a pattern seen in the 1920s, 1930, and 1954—after every major period of antireligious activity by the state, official condemnations of "excesses" were lodged. The 1964 declaration is almost as strong as what is being said during the *glasnost* period. But the level of contrition was not matched by actions. Most of the churches closed under Khrushchev remain closed under his successors. The laws written to imprison and intimidate believers were not only left on the books but often utilized. And though there was less physical violence against believers than before, hostility continued in countless ways throughout the next two decades.

One important difference between the 1965 admission of past wrongdoing and the admission at the end of the 1980s is that the latter has been made public. Millions of people, not only in the Soviet Union but also in the West, have read the *glasnost*-era confessions of past misconduct.

SOVIET CHURCHMEN AND THE TRUTH ABOUT PERSECUTION

The first half of the 1960s witnessed a masterful coup in Soviet disinformation. The Soviet authorities managed simultaneously to crack down on religion at home and to score public relations points abroad for their religious tolerance in letting registered Soviet leaders travel abroad.

The Orthodox pointman for Soviet propaganda about religion during the Khrushchev campaign was Nikodim. He was just thirty-one when he became the head of the Department of External Ecclesiastical Relations in 1960, following Nikolai's demise in the wake of his mild protest at the Kremlin. Nikodim later became bishop, archbishop, and finally the Metropolitan of Leningrad. Though Nikodim articulated the Party line on foreign policy and "religious freedom," he must be seen as a complex figure. He had become a Christian as a teenager and had grown up amidst the stark realities of a society dominated by an antireligious government.

Whatever the justification (or lack of it) for the disinformation Nikodim spread at international church meetings, the naivete and gullibility of his Western listeners is even more disconcerting. Pospielovsky once asked Nikodim about the false statements he and other Russian bishops made in public; Nikodim replied with a "sad smile":

> It is you in the West who react so readily to untrue statements. . . . The Soviet public has got used to them. . . . I am not saying that this is good or bad, I am merely stating the fact that what shocks you here does not evoke a similar response in our country.

There are two problems with a lie. The first is in telling it; the second is in believing it when we ought to know better. In the case of Soviet religious propaganda, the telling has frequently been the product of considerable outside pressure; the believing has all too often been the result of ignorance and laziness.

III. Brezhnev to Gorbachev

The period from 1964 to 1985 is more difficult to define than previous periods in Soviet history. The concerted attack on the church ended, though numerous incidents of violence against individual believers continued. It was as if both church and state settled into a long holding pattern characterized by continued persecution of the unregistered believers and continued discrimination and harassment of the registered.

No story better epitomizes the hopes, dilemmas, and tragedies of the Christian church in a hostile atheist sea than that of Father Dmitry Dudko. Anyone harboring illusions that persecution was confined to Lenin or Stalin or Khrushchev will discover in Dudko's wrenching biography evidence that persecution lasted right into the 1980s, to the very threshold of Gorbachev's rise to power. Nor did Dudko's international reputation save him from the humiliating and degrading treatment he was to receive at the hands of the state. The fate of the thousands unknown to the West has often been much worse.

THE TRAGEDY OF FATHER DUDKO

Father Dudko was in his late thirties when he was ordained a priest in 1960. He had already endured more than eight-and-a-half years in labor camps under Stalin for having had in his possession religious poetry. He began to attract attention in the early 1960s because of his unusually warm and effective ministry at the Church of St. Nicholas in Moscow. Natalia Solzhenitsyn described why people from all over Moscow came to his services and sought contact with him:

> After every encounter with him you are left with the feeling: how deep and joyful is his faith! He is a man of surprising integrity and simplicity, and his preaching finds a direct and accurate path to a person's heart.

It was inevitable that such a successful pastor would disturb the Communist authorities. In September 1972 Dudko was told that he was going to be stripped of his parish. In untypical fashion, the next Sunday he informed his congregation of his impending dismissal, asked for their help, and even expressed the likelihood that there were people present (informers) to disturb the internal affairs of the church. The authorities delayed following through on their threat.

Father Dudko is best known for the remarkable discussion sessions he held at his church beginning in December 1973. His purpose was to give people an opportunity to ask questions about theology, the church, and faith.

The response to these sessions was electric. Raised in an atheist society, with little religious literature available, people were starved to hear what a man of God had to say about the atheist notions with which they were constantly deluged. Dudko became a highly skilled and effective apologist of Christian truths. Youth in particular were drawn to the dynamic priest. By early 1974, his conversations were known throughout Moscow and beyond.

A good way to gain insight into how his activities were perceived by the authorities is to read "The Furov Report." This paper was prepared for the Communist party Central Committee in 1975 by V. Furov, a deputy chairman of the Council for Religious Affairs (CRA). In addition to citing Dudko's earlier "crimes" which landed him in Stalin's labor camps, Furov contends that Father Dudko "continued to write libelous materials and preach slanderous sermons, train young people in dangerous ideology, and collect and disseminate *samizdat* and other literature from abroad."

Dudko, the report contends, has been warned about his "antisocial activity" and his ideological work with young people; but he has refused to change his behavior.

Patriarch Pimen was enlisted by the authorities in May 1974 to prohibit Dudko from preaching at the church in Moscow. In September he was transferred to the village of Kobanovo, fifty miles out of Moscow. Further, Dudko signed a pledge to avoid sermon topics which might be interpreted as political. However, he continued to attract more and more people to the church. A decision was made to deal with Dudko more forcibly. In March 1975 he was involved in a serious and suspicious accident, which left him with two broken legs. The militia refused to go to the scene of the accident, and no charges were filed.

In April 1977, the authorities launched their next missile at the pesky priest—two issues of the nationally prominent journal *Literary Gazette* contained attacks not only on Dudko, but on three other prominent Orthodox figures: Gleb Yakunin, Lev Regelson, and Alexander Ogorodnikov. On April 27, the four gathered at Dudko's Moscow apartment to protest to the Western press that the allegations of "anti-Soviet" slander were absolutely false.

At the end of the year the church hierarchy once again responded to an order from the CRA and dismissed Dudko from his parish. His congregation protested vigorously, but to no avail. His new parish, in Grebnevo, was a full two hours from Moscow.

Next the authorities sought to frighten Dudko by going after one of his three children. Mikhail, just seventeen years old, was subjected in December 1977 to an involuntary psychiatric examination, a frequent precursor of compulsory incarceration in a psychiatric hospital. Mikhail was not imprisoned, nor did his father cease his infectious Christian apologetics. In November of 1978, Dudko began printing a parish newsletter called *In the Light of the Transfiguration*. It focused on religious topics but also reported on the authorities' harassment of church members.

In June 1978, the militia invaded the building next to Father Dudko's church (where he occasionally spent the night), threatened to shoot everyone, and dragged out one of Dudko's followers. The young man, dressed only in his underwear, was pistol whipped in the snow. The militia took him in but refused to treat his injuries.

The young people, however, continued to make the lengthy journey to Grebnevo to hear the engaging priest. Finally, the authorities decided to take Dudko into custody. There seemed no other way to stop his ministry; nothing frightens the authorities more than churchmen capable of conveying to young people an attractive view of religion. Father Dudko's direct, open style was quietly and calmly destroying the stereotypes of atheist propaganda about what it means to be a believer.

The morning of January 15, 1980, twelve KGB officers arrived to take Dudko into custody. Within a few hours he was in the dreaded Lefortovo prison in Moscow. Though many both in the Soviet Union and abroad were quick to protest, Dudko's own church hierarchy was not among them. Archbishop Pitirim of the Moscow Patriarchate could not avoid fielding questions in Stockholm about the imprisoned priest. Pitirim, however, recalled that he had been in seminary in 1945 with Dudko, whom he remembered as a "nervous and unbalanced person." Metropolitan Alexy of Tallinn, while traveling in Austria, noted: "In the Soviet Union, citizens are never arrested for their religious or ideological convictions."

No one knows exactly what happened between that January morning when Dudko was arrested and June 5 when he signed a recantation for his "anti-Soviet" activities. We do know that his public confession disappointed and divided his followers and left Dudko disoriented and lonely. One of the spiritual heroes of the late Soviet period had apparently been broken by his interrogators.

Dudko's confession was orchestrated by Soviet authorities to get the maximum domestic and foreign coverage. The full text was published in Izvestiia on June 21, 1980, the day after the television recantation was seen by millions of Soviets. Dudko asserted that he was "arrested not for believing in God but for crime." His confession focused on his alleged role in bringing church and state into conflict in the Soviet Union, and his part in providing information to the West which discredited his country. "I renounce what I have done, and I regard my so called struggle with godlessness as a struggle with Soviet power."

The day after his televised confession, Dudko was released from custody and allowed to return home. Over the next few months he wrote and said many things which indicated that he was in a state of considerable anguish. On July 27 he wrote the following in a letter to his "spiritual children."

> I cannot forgive myself for my weakness, and my heart is torn asunder seeing your confusion and hearing garbled interpretations. I shudder at the thought of how I must appear to everyone, into what temptation I have led people, how I have disheartened those whom I had previously heartened. I prostrate myself before you and beg for your forgiveness.

He also expressed surprise that people did not read between the lines of his confession.

Dudko's confession compelled many to speculate not only about what had happened to him, but to wonder if the same thing could happen to them. Some sought to guard in advance against being compromised in the future. Irina Zalesskaia wrote: "If I should make a similar 'confession' or renounce my views, I ask that this be considered the result of physical or psychological torture."

I have given considerable space to one man's drama in hopes that we can better grasp what it has meant to serve God in this Communist country. That a gifted man, one of the most skilled communicators of Christian truths to the secular Soviet world of our day, could be reduced to denouncing his nonpolitical religious activities as crimes is itself a crime against the human spirit. It is a crime that has been committed repeatedly in every decade of Communist rule in this troubled land.

In 1981 the criminal charges against Dudko were formally dropped due to his age and his "repentance." But for many others the charges were not dropped. During most of the seventies the number of known Christian prisoners averaged about one hundred. But the wave of arrests in the late seventies and early eighties swelled the number to at least three hundred, about the average during the Khrushchev assault on religion in the first half of the sixties.

CONCLUSION

On the eve of Mikhail Gorbachev's rise to power in 1985, the conflict and tension between church and state were still very noticeable. Although battered and bloodied, the Christian faith in a variety of denominational forms had survived concerted efforts to weaken or destroy it.

Two different conceptions of the role of religion in society continued to be at odds. There was the Marxist view that religion was a kind of opium, a foreign substance that caused great harm in the society. And there was the Christian notion that religion was essential to society's very survival. As Gleb Yakunin put it: "Religion is like salt which protects humanity from decomposition and disintegration. Any attempt to banish it from social life invariably leads to a degradation of society."

That is the essence of the debate: Is religion a society's opium or its salt? And can a society that has viewed religion as an opium for seven decades begin to view it as salt, or at least as an element that poses no threat?

PART II

THE GORBACHEV ERA AND BEYOND

PROLOGUE

GLASNOST, *PERESTROIKA*, AND THE DEATH OF AN IDEOLOGY

To go not knowing where; to bring back not knowing what.
                                                    Russian proverb

*A*s the 1990s unfold the euphoria of the 1980s is giving way to a feeling of unease and uncertainty in the Soviet Union. There is a specter of chaos and even civil war which is sometimes overlooked by foreign observers.

An embattled Gorbachev has struggled to ride the whirlwind, but shows signs of weariness. There is a myth in the West that if we just knew enough about Gorbachev, if we could just get inside his head, we could determine exactly what he believes and what he intends to do. It seems to have escaped us that his views may be in transition and that he may often not know what he will do next. This is a more likely explanation for the sudden shifts in policy which have taken place on his watch, and are likely to continue.

Events in Eastern Europe and the Soviet Union have often tumbled far ahead of what Gorbachev anticipated, and he has frequently had to jump forward to not be left behind. The great reformer now finds himself in the unpleasant position of having to watch Russian republic parliamentarians push ahead on an agenda often more radical than his own.

One of the ironies of the present situation is the difference between Gorbachev's perspective on Marxist-Leninism, at least his public position on it, and the much more critical perspective he is allowing others to express. Nor has Marxist-Leninist ideology ever been lower in the public esteem than it is now. In October 1989, the head of the All-Union Komsomol (youth organization), announced that ten million had abandoned the organization during the past four years. Circulation for Pravda, the Communist party official newspaper, has dropped from 10.7 million in 1985 to half a million by the fall of 1990. The Communist party suffered a net loss of 600,000 members between January and October 1990, leaving a total membership of 17.7 million. In June 1990, a poll conducted by the Party itself confirmed that less than half those polled considered the Communist party to be "the leading force" in Soviet society. Long before *glasnost*, Marxism had lost its hold on the Soviet Union's masses; now it has lost even the vast majority of its public defenders. Since 1990, Soviet university students are no longer required to take mandatory courses or exams in Marxist-Leninism.

In May 1990, *World Marxist Review* (English title), announced that it was ceasing its publication. This Soviet-controlled, Prague-based journal was founded in 1958 and at one time its editorial board included members from sixty-nine Communist parties. In its heyday it was published in thirty-seven languages (often under the title of *Problems of Peace and Socialism*), distributed to 500,000 people in 145 countries. A more graphic example of the collapse of world Marxism is not to be found.

GORBACHEV'S PERSPECTIVE

According to Mikhail Gorbachev, *perestroika* is "a policy of accelerating the country's social and economic progress and renewing all spheres of life." Throughout his book, *Perestroika*, which he was asked to write by an American publisher, Gorbachev insists that though economic renewal is a key ingredient in *perestroika*, the ultimate purpose is "a thorough renewal of every aspect of Soviet life."

Perestroika is required, asserts Gorbachev, because beginning in the late 1970s the Soviet economy began to stagnate. "Economic failures became more frequent," and "a gradual erosion of the ideological and moral values of our people began."

This unhappy state of affairs, according to the Soviet leader, is emphatically not because socialism has failed, as some in the West believe. Rather it has occurred because the potential of socialism has not been realized. The solution, therefore, is to return to the legacy of Vladimir Lenin.

The general secretary dates the general shift of policy to April 1985, just a month after his own election by the Central Committee to the top position in the Communist party. He believes that the Central Committee's adoption in June 1987 of "Fundamentals of Radical Restructuring of Economic Management" may be the most important economic reform in the Soviet Union since 1921, when Lenin launched his New Economic Policy.

Historians have widely interpreted Lenin's 1920s plan as a concession towards capitalism in order to allow the economy to recover from the Civil War. Like Lenin, however, Gorbachev has repeatedly assured faithful Communists that his actions are not in any way a retreat from socialist ideals or goals.

In addition to returning to Lenin, Gorbachev emphasizes two other ways of furthering *perestroika*: *glasnost* and democratization. The former is directly related to the mobilization of the "human factor," which is not possible apart from a new openness. There is an assumption that the success of *perestroika* is directly tied to the individual and whether his noneconomic needs are met.

Gorbachev contends that many of the Soviet Union's problems exist because democratic processes were not allowed to develop. This must not be allowed to continue: "We need broad democratization of all aspects of society." That democratization is also the main guarantee that the current processes are irreversible.

Has Gorbachev changed his views on Marx and Lenin since *Perestroika* was first published in 1987? In November 1989, Gorbachev told a forum of Soviet students that the USSR's problems are the fault of the "deformations of socialism" by Stalin and Brezhnev, and ought not to be traced to Marx or Lenin. In February 1990, he assured the Central Committee that democratic socialism relies "on the great legacy of Marx, Engels and Lenin." Nevertheless, judging by Gorbachev's about-face on multiparty democracy, it would be a mistake to consider his position to be set in cement. Nor is it clear to what degree Gorbachev feels politically constrained at this time not to question the patron saints of communism. He may one day feel compelled to renounce them.

THE PUBLIC DISMANTLING OF MARXIST-LENINISM

We still adhere to Marxist theory, but much of this theory should be adjusted because many of the conclusions of Marx have failed to stand the test of time.

What is particularly startling about these words is their source. They belong to Oleg Bogomolov, the director of what was then called the Institute of the Economics of the World Socialist System, and they were spoken on February 8, 1989 at a press conference of the Soviet Foreign Ministry.

Bogomolov also asserted that the USSR's decision to ban private property had undermined the farmer's concern for the land. He predicted that changes in Soviet law would legalize family farms and allow the farmer to select his own crops and sell them at market value. He also conceded that "the Stalinist system . . . was imposed on other countries," and he suggested that the time had come for each country to find its own way to recover from the damage done.

Bogomolov's words of early 1989 turned out to be almost prophetic. Indeed, it was time for "each country to find its own way to recover from the damage done." By the end of the year, the face of Eastern Europe had been radically transformed with Communists everywhere running for cover or changing their party name. Little wonder that in 1990 Bogomolov's institute changed its name to the Institute of Eastern Europe and Foreign Policy Studies.

But even before the fall of Eastern Europe, other scholars were going well beyond Bogomolov. The charge has been led by Alexander Tsipko, a consultant to the Communist Party Central Committee in 1988 and 1989, and since the beginning of 1990, the deputy director of the Institute of Eastern Europe and Foreign Policy Studies. Alexander Yakovlev, the most progressive member of the Politburo, is reported to be close to Tsipko and has had wide exposure to his ideas.

While still an advisor to the Central Committee, Tsipko dropped a bombshell with a four-part article published in *Science and Life* which asserted that the roots of Stalin's purges ought to be sought in the Bolshevik terror immediately following the October Revolution. He charged that the flaws of Marxist theory produced Stalinism. Even earlier, in May 1988, economic journalist Vasily Selyunin asserted in the pages of the prestigious *Novyi Mir* (New World) that Lenin had taken a step backwards from the capitalist system, set up a system of forced labor and concentration camps, and returned to the use of "slavery."

Tsipko went so far as to contend that Marxist attacks on the marketplace inevitably result in "totalitarianism, in the violation of the rights and dignity of individuals, and in the creation of an omnipotent administrative and bureaucratic apparatus." Tsipko ridiculed the position long maintained by moderates and liberals in the Soviet Union (and the West) that the problem with Stalin was simply the methods he used to achieve worthwhile ends. According to this Soviet scholar, Stalin was no aberration from Marxism; his hostility to the independent peasant was basic to classical Marxism. Then Tsipko poses the question which many thought could never appear in print in the USSR: Was collectivism even a good idea?

> When the ideas about the goals of socialism are wrong ... if they contradict the laws of normal civil life, it is useless to argue about the pace or methods by which they are achieved. When you are dealing with an unrealistic goal, it does not matter whether you try to achieve it by cavalry methods or gradually—the result will be the same.

Tsipko's analysis strikes at the very heart of Marxist communism—its view of human nature. In a published article in 1989 he declared: "All our absurdities stem from our dogged refusal to see man as he really is, as he has been created by nature and by history." Marx believed that the abolition of private property would end social conflict, but instead repression was fostered in pursuit of an ideal society. Tsipko believes that Soviet society is in a state of "moral infantilism," because by "telling man he is an angel, but treating him like a child" citizens have seen their individual conscience atrophy and have lost their sense of personal responsibility for their actions.

Nor does Tsipko shy away from proposing a means to escape the present economic and moral crisis. On a trip abroad in February 1990 he argued that without a revival of Christian beliefs, renewal in Soviet society was inconceivable. In an effort to foster renewal, Tsipko is editing a reprint of the famous 1909 symposium of essays titled Vekhi (Landmarks). The collection is notable in that former Marxists (such as Nikolai Berdyaev and Sergei Bulgakov) predict that the ideas of Marx, atheism, and materialism will lead to disastrous results for society. They advocate a return to Christian or religious understandings of man and society.

* * * *

The Soviet Union is now in the cauldron of dramatic societal changes. The old Marxist-Leninist ideology is on its death bed, though no one yet knows which dogmas and values will take its place.

What has changed, and what has not, since Gorbachev became

the leader of the Soviet Union? Have *glasnost* and *perestroika* made any significant impact on Soviet society and the church? The chapters that follow will help answer these questions and look at prospects for the future. Finally, some recommendations will be made for how Western Christians ought to respond to the unique opportunities the present moment provides.

CHAPTER 3

THE INFORMATION MONOLITH:
DAMAGED BEYOND REPAIR

IDEAS AND INFORMATION:
TRADITIONALLY A SOVIET STATE MONOPOLY

An American and a Soviet were arguing one day about the relative freedoms of their respective countries. "My country is so free," bragged the American, "that I can stand in front of the White House and criticize the president of the United States as much as I want—even have my protest aired on national TV—and nothing will happen to me."

"That's not such a big deal," responded the Soviet. "I can stand in front of the Kremlin and say anything I want about the president of the United States, too, and nothing will happen to me either."

*T*his bit of Russian humor points to the sobering reality that, since 1917, Soviet control of its people has been based on two things: physical coercion and the control of information. Too little attention has been paid to the latter in our studies of the Soviet Union.

This is only natural. After all, the Soviet Union's terrorization of millions of its citizens produced a wave of graphic stories of suffering, death, and human courage. We know something of the awesome power the USSR has employed to insure the obedience or at least passivity of its people. We are much less aware of how crucial the control of information is for manipulating the minds of the population.

Soviet schools have typically displayed on their walls anti-religious posters which depict believers as superstitious and ignorant. From the earliest grades reason and religion were presented as at odds. A well-known poster pictured a Soviet cosmonaut in space, hand to forehead scanning the limitless horizon, with the caption: "No God!" Of course, in the Soviet schools and media no alternative perspectives were provided. No Christians were permitted to give their views on whether science and the Bible are really at war with each other. No priest or pastor was allowed to present his version of what the church believes about God and the world.

Article 52 of the Soviet Constitution, which allegedly guarantees the right of religious worship, makes crystal clear the State's exclusive access to the public through the media on matters of religion. Antireligious propaganda is specifically guaranteed, with no similar right provided for believers. Scientific Marxism risks no argument about its "reasonable and empirically grounded" worldview.

A typical tack taken against troublesome local believers—such as those who refused to agree to the restrictive state regulations governing the Church—was to vilify them in print. Their patriotism, intelligence, and morality have been pilloried for decades. They have often been accused of conspiring with foreign intelligence networks. Those who were publicly defamed have had no legal right to respond or defend themselves in print to the millions of readers exposed to the State-sponsored attacks.

There can be no question about it: the control of the press is a powerful and deadly weapon in the hands of an antireligious government.

For many decades the Soviet Union has coveted its control of information. It has properly understood that a free and independent press and an uncontrolled literary culture represent a threat to its monopoly of information and perspective.

In the late 1970s I had an opportunity to hear a Communist viewpoint on these matters firsthand. A Party member from Moscow State University asked me to give my frank reactions to living in the Soviet Union. "What have you been most struck by while working here these past five months?"

I thought for a moment and then replied, "The control of information. I am surprised by the extent to which Soviet citizens are not allowed to read other points of view. In the university where I am a graduate student in the United States, I can go to my library and read *Pravda, Izvestiia,* and virtually any book or periodical the Soviet Union publishes, but your citizens do not have the right to read *Time,* the *Washington Post,* or the *New York Times.* Nor do your students know the most basic, indisputable facts about the Stalin era."

The eyes of the Communist party member flashed, and he declared with unusual frankness: "What's the point of reopening old debates? Besides if we gave people a choice, they would want to return to capitalism. And as for Stalin, there is no point in dredging up all that old history. The people are children, and we must control what information they have."

That comment was made seven years before Gorbachev came to power, and it reflects well the Party's traditional attitude toward the control of information. Nor is it a view that has been finally and unquestionably defeated in the Soviet Union today. It is, however, being seriously challenged by some at the highest levels of government and Party.

STOPPING THE JAMMING

As significant as are the changes in the way religion is treated in Soviet literature and the press is what people are allowed to hear about it from outside sources.

The *New York Times* reports that before the Soviets stopped jamming, they were estimated to be spending more than a billion dollars a year to block foreign radio transmissions into their country. The USSR has probably spent far more on jamming Western programming than the West has spent on producing and transmitting it. Despite the Soviet's best efforts, however, considerable Western programming has reached Soviet shortwave radios.

According to Mark Elliott, director of the Institute for the Study of Christianity and Marxism (Wheaton College), in early 1988 over 360 hours a week of religious broadcasting was being transmitted into the Soviet Union. Since jamming was frequently sporadic and aimed primarily at the Western government-sponsored broadcasts, much religious broadcasting got through, particularly when it confined itself to nonpolitical religious subject matter.

As late as 1987, a detailed article giving the standard denunciation of Western broadcasting appeared in the Soviet serial *Questions of Scientific Atheism.* The programming was described as politically reactionary and anti-Soviet and a tool of carefully coordinated religious propaganda which, in addition to talking about

God, criticized the lack of spirituality in Soviet society.

In January 1988 the Soviets ceased jamming the BBC. In May of that year they stopped interfering with Voice of America, and in late November the last jammed foreign broadcast, Radio Liberty, was allowed to transmit freely. Radio Liberty is funded by the U.S. government and broadcasts into the Soviet Union in twelve languages to an estimated sixteen million listeners. It was praised even in Moscow newspapers for having better coverage of the December 1988 Armenian earthquake than did their own media.

The timing of the decision to cease jamming was not accidental. Moscow was actively seeking Western support for its bid to host an international human rights conference in 1991. By the end of 1988, it had won support from its fellow members of the Commission for Security and Cooperation in Europe who were meeting in Vienna when the jamming stopped. Unfortunately, interfering with the air waves is not entirely a thing of the past. In March 1989 a Radio Liberty broadcast on a demonstration in Moscow was jammed, as was an interview with a member of the Christian Democratic Union.

The decision to cease jamming is a tangible sign that *glasnost* is not just window dressing. It will not only make it easier for Soviet citizens to gain information on both internal and external matters, thus forcing the Soviet press to be more responsible, but it will provide new opportunities for religious programming to reach the ears of believers and nonbelievers alike. This is a significant step toward religious freedom.

THE RECOVERY OF THE PAST

Memory is returning to us. It is returning in the form of books that previously went unpublished.

These words appeared in August 1988 in the introduction to a Soviet edition of the *Memoirs* of Nadezhda Mandelstam, which recounts the suffering and confusion of the 1930s. Similar firsthand accounts told previously often led to fresh encounters with the Gulag.

For many years Boris Pasternak's *Dr. Zhivago* has circulated in the Soviet underground. Not considered nearly as dangerous as Solzhenitsyn's works, *Dr. Zhivago* nevertheless was unsettling to the authorities because its depiction of the early months and years of the Revolution raised questions about whether or not the lofty ideals of the revolutionaries were swept aside early on by narrowness and cruelty.

In 1958 the important Soviet journal *Novyi Mir* (New World) refused to publish *Dr. Zhivago*. The editors later explained to the author their reasons for rejecting his work: "The spirit of your novel is the spirit of rejection of the Socialist Revolution. . . . We cannot even consider the publication of your novel." Thirty years later, *Novyi Mir* published *Dr. Zhivago*.

Another taboo topic for the Soviet Union has been why committed Communists have sometimes abandoned their Communist convictions. Thus, Arthur Koestler's *Darkness at Noon* (1941) was not published in Russian and was forbidden reading material. In this fascinating novel, the English writer speculates on why completely loyal Bolsheviks confessed in the 1930s to crimes they never committed. Koestler argues that blind, indiscriminate loyalty to Communist ideology warped the minds and judgment of true Bolshevik believers. Furthermore their willingness to lie constantly for the "good of the Party" eventually robbed them of their ability to distinguish between truth and falsehood.

In July 1988, the literary magazine *Neva* began publishing *Darkness at Noon*. The Soviet introduction does not agree with Koestler's rejection of communism, but it argues that Koestler's decision was understandable and Soviet readers should be acquainted with the book.

The Soviet Union has made a habit of condemning its own creative citizens, even those who have gained the most prestigious literary honor the world has to offer. Pasternak could not leave the Soviet Union in 1958 to receive the Nobel Prize for fear that Khrushchev would not let him back into the country. Solzhenitsyn's Nobel Prize of 1970 was followed four years later by his expulsion from the Soviet Union.

In 1963 a Leningrad newspaper carried a major attack on a poet in his early twenties. "It's time to stop coddling this literary parasite. There is no place in Leningrad for the likes of Brodsky." The next year, Joseph Brodsky was arrested for "parasitism" and sent to labor camp. Following his emigration in 1972, Brodsky was awarded the Nobel Prize in 1987 for his poetry.

But during *glasnost*, Brodsky and other formerly forbidden writers are being perceived differently. In 1989 two *Izvestiia* correspondents filed a story on Brodsky which noted that articles about his unfair trial were being planned:

If we really want to move forward, not just in word but in

deed, don't we have to evaluate ourselves? When should we do it, if not today? And not merely for self-purification or repentance (we have the knack of repenting and then sinning all over again), but so that in the future it will be impossible, or at least more difficult, to decide someone's fate so drastically.

Brodsky was just one of Khrushchev's victims. There were millions more under Stalin. Does *glasnost* extend to a discussion of their fates?

EXORCISING A DEMON: FACING THE TRUTH ABOUT STALIN

Some events in life sear themselves into our memories. For one man those memories involve reliving numerous truck rides several miles out of town to the top of a hill. "We'd shout, Come on out! Line up!' They get out, and in front of them 'there's a pit dug for them. They'd get out and start huddling closer together, and we'd immediately open fire."

The words are those of one of Stalin's executioners from Omsk, and they were recorded in a late 1988 issue of the Soviet journal *Moscow News*. In 1937 and 1938 alone, according to Solzhenitsyn, 1.7 million may have been executed. Even more died in labor camps, and millions more perished in the mass terror against the peasantry between 1930 and 1934. Hitler has been the embodiment of evil for most people, yet Joseph Stalin was responsible for the death of far more of his own citizens than was Hitler. In a 1989 article in the Soviet periodical *Arguments and Facts,* dissident Soviet historian Roy Medvedev estimates that Stalin was responsible for about twenty million deaths in labor camps, executions, forced collectivization, and deliberately induced famines.

Many facets of the Stalin years are being rewritten. In the fall of 1989, Soviet historian Stalinislav Kulchitsky estimated in a Soviet newspaper that nine million people died in the Ukrainian famine of 1933 directly as a result of Stalin's policies. The following February a resolution of the Ukrainian Communist Party called the Ukrainian famine of 1932-33 a "national tragedy" and laid the blame for it on Stalin's "criminal" policies of collectivization. They also called for publication of articles and archival materials on the topic. Nor has Stalin escaped blame for at least some of the staggering World War II losses sustained by the Soviet military. In June 1989, an article in *Pravda* charged that it was Stalin's "gross mistakes" and ignoring of intelligence reports of Hitler's impending attack which led to the

Soviet Union's initial defeats in the war. The article was released on the forty-eighth anniversary of the German invasion.

One of the most startling revelations of the Gorbachev era has been that 3.5 million people were executed under Stalin, half of them between 1937 and 1938. This is the highest number yet given by Soviet authorities, and the admission came from the KGB itself. These figures confirm those given by Solzhenitsyn. Two years earlier a Soviet newspaper reported that a secret memorandum to Stalin had just been made available. It was from his minister of state security, Semen Ignatev, and it stated that in 1953 there were twelve million in Soviet labor camps.

In mid-August 1990 Gorbachev issued his most sweeping decree to date on the crimes of the Stalin-era. He called for a restoration of all civil rights to the surviving victims of Stalin's policies and he called on all the USSR's fifteen republic legislatures to come up with specific proposals on how to implement the decree. Crimes condemned by Gorbachev included cruel repression of ethnic and religious groups, forced collectivization of the peasantry, mass deportations and executions.

The Soviets are even showing some openness to publishing the views of the most prominent Western experts on the Stalin period. In early 1989 an interview with Robert Conquest, author of *The Great Terror* and *Harvest of Sorrow*, appeared in *Moscow News*. The introductory comments noted that shortly after *The Great Terror* was published in the West in 1968, it reached the Soviet Union through *samizdat* and was immediately recognized by the Soviet intelligentsia as "one of the most important Western research works on Soviet history." The Leningrad journal *Neva* plans to publish Conquest's work on Stalin, with introductory remarks by Medvedev.

It is ironic that Conquest has been praised in the Soviet press in recent months for scholarly work that earned him only disdain from Western religious and political leftists and peace activists. For two decades they have belittled his research and accused his work of fueling the Cold War.

The dismantling of Stalin is also occurring through the powerful medium of the stage. In February 1989 Muscovites were treated to the opening of a new play, *The Hard Route*, based on the memoirs of Eugenia Ginzburg. The audience responded with a fifteen-minute standing ovation at the end of the premiere of the bitterly anti-Stalinist play.

The new openness toward Stalin began sometime around the spring of 1987. Within a few months two of the most *glasnost*-oriented Soviet periodicals, *Ogonek* and *Moscow News*, along with prominent cultural figures and some dissidents, founded the Memorial Society to help the Soviet populace come to grips with a past the textbooks and authorities have pretended never happened. In June 1988 Gorbachev expressed his support for the idea of a memorial in honor of Stalin's victims.

For nine extraordinary days in November 1988, more than thirty-five thousand Soviet citizens filed silently through an exhibit in Moscow devoted to Stalin's repressions. They stood and gazed, some with tears in their eyes, at a bulletin board which gave information on the disappearances and deaths of loved ones—a few of the countless millions driven into the infamous prison camps dotting the Soviet landscape. By the time the exhibition closed, more than 50,000 roubles ($80,000) had been deposited in a wheelbarrow for the construction of a research complex and a permanent memorial dedicated to the victims of Stalin's crimes.

THE INDOMITABLE SOLZHENITSYN

One hundred years from now historians may well write that the person who best epitomizes the victory of the Russian religious spirit over Soviet communism is Alexander Solzhenitsyn.

Himself a veteran of the gulags, Solzhenitsyn's relentless effort to tell the truth about the Soviet past resulted in his exile to the West in 1974. In 1989 he completed one of the most monumental historical/literary efforts in history—the five-thousand page cycle of historical novels called *The Red Wheel*, and covering the period 1914-22. So far only the first work, *August 1914*, is available in English. Solzhenitsyn is obsessed with giving his Russian soulmates the gift of history—their history with all its pains and sorrows, but also with its traditions and hopes. And much of its hope, Solzhenitsyn believes, rests on recovering and nurturing the religious depths of Russian culture.

Perhaps the most dramatic sign of *glasnost* in the Soviet Union is the publication of Solzhenitsyn's *Gulag Archipelago*, his monumental study of Stalin's labor camps. This is particularly unusual in that the authorities have considered no author more subversive in past decades than Solzhenitsyn.

What has particularly disturbed the Soviets is not that

Solzhenitsyn has provided voluminous documentation of Stalin's crimes, but that he has laid them at Lenin's doorstep. Lenin and Marx have almost always been preserved from official criticism in the Soviet Union. Even when Khrushchev and Gorbachev have attacked the excesses of Stalin, they have been careful to insist that Stalin departed from the Leninist path.

In contrast, Solzhenitsyn asserts that the seeds of Stalin's excesses are to be found in Lenin's conception of a narrow Party. He also believes that a departure from religion, from God, is bound to lead a country into great crimes. The dogmatic atheist Marx, according to Solzhenitsyn, cannot escape responsibility for what has happened in the Soviet Union.

In the summer of 1988, Sergei Zalygin, editor of *Novyi Mir*, was ready to publish *Cancer Ward* and *The First Circle*, but Solzhenitsyn balked. The feisty author, who has lived in Vermont since his exile, insisted that *Gulag* be published first. But now trouble came from another quarter—the Central Committee's ideology department. Bypassing the editor, the department placed a phone call directly to the printer to destroy two million copies of the October issue of *Novyi Mir*. The back of the cover advertised upcoming publications of Solzhenitsyn in the journal.

As late as November 1988, prospects for publishing Solzhenitsyn's most controversial works were very much in doubt. At a meeting of senior editors, the Party chief of ideology, Vadim Medvedev, declared his opposition to the publication of *Gulag* and *Lenin in Zurich*. He charged that the negative treatment of Lenin and the October Revolution would "undermine the foundations on which today's life rests."

Not long before Medvedev's comments, a small newspaper in Ukraine published Solzhenitsyn's 1974 essay "Live Not by Lies." Shortly after that, two Baltic newspapers reprinted the article, and then in February 1989 it appeared in a Moscow periodical. The editor of the Moscow paper describes Solzhenitsyn as "the greatest Russian writer of today" and insists that it makes no sense to ban any of his works.

The decision to finally take all of Solzhenitsyn's works off the forbidden list did not come easily. For six months Zalygin submitted galleys of Solzhenitsyn's Nobel Prize lecture and each time the censors refused to allow publication. In fact, Gorbachev himself may have been one of the last obstacles to *glasnost* on this issue. The underground publication *Referendum* reported that Zalygin had a personal conversation with Gorbachev in which it became clear that the Soviet leader was irritated with Solzhenitsyn's negative opinions about Lenin. In the opinion of Western Soviet experts, Gorbachev finally decided to reverse the ban on the Russian writer because Gorbachev's resistance was irritating liberal allies of his reform program, there was an outpouring of public protest to the Central Committee regarding the censorship of *Novyi Mir*, and bits and pieces of Solzhenitsyn were cropping up in print repeatedly as publishers found ways to avoid the censors. By the spring of 1989, the final decision was made; there would be no further obstacles to the publication of Solzhenitsyn's works in the USSR.

By September 1989, the unbelievable moment had finally arrived; 1.5 million copies of the first portions of *Gulag Archipelago* appeared in *Novyi Mir*. Only one-third of the *Gulag* appeared in the journal, but an agreement was worked out with the "Sovetsky Pisatel" (Soviet Writer) publishing house for the release of several more volumes of Solzhenitsyn, including a complete three-volume version of *Gulag*. In addition, plans are in the works for all subscribers to the journal (already exploding to 2.5 million by the spring of 1990) to have the opportunity to purchase a special seven-volume edition of Solzhenitsyn's collected works. As one member of the editorial board of *Literaturnaya Gazeta* (Literary Gazette) put it, the publication of *Gulag Archipelago* is "the most notable event in the literary life" of the USSR in 1989.

In July 1989 the USSR Writers' Union voted unanimously to rescind its 1969 expulsion of Solzhenitsyn from its ranks. It also called its members who were deputies to the USSR Supreme Soviet to work for a revocation of the 1974 Supreme Soviet decree depriving Solzhenitsyn of his citizenship and his right to live in the USSR. On August 16, 1990, Gorbachev issued a decree restoring Solzhenitsyn's citizenship, as well as that of twenty-two other human rights activists and artists exiled during the Brezhnev era. The family, however, wants the charge of "treason" to be repealed also.

It is hard to overestimate the historical and political significance of the publication of *Gulag* in the Soviet Union. In symbolic terms, it represents something like the removal of the Berlin Wall. It means the old ideology with its totalitarian control of information is a thing of the past. It means new opportunities for religious perspectives to help inform and shape the future of what has been the Soviet Union. For where the government has a monopoly on information there can be no democracy and there can be no freedom of religion.

CHAPTER 4

RELIGION IN SOVIET CULTURE:
STIRRINGS OF NEW LIFE

*I*n his 1986 short story, Place of Action, well-known Soviet writer Victor Astafev describes a beautiful and moving celebration of Christ's resurrection as the author experienced it as a youth. He then describes this same occasion being "celebrated" in the present by a group of drunk and crude Soviet fishermen. The stark contrast troubles him:

> What has happened with us? Who and for which transgressions has plunged us into this abyss of evil and misfortunes? Who has extinguished the light of virtue in our souls . . . the sacred light of our consciousness. We used to live with light in our souls . . . without scratching out the eyes of our neighbors, without breaking our neighbor's bones. Why has all this been abducted from us, and replaced by godlessness? . . . To whom are we going to turn our prayers now . . . to ask forgiveness? . . . Yet, in the past . . . we used to forgive even our enemies.

SOVIET LITERATURE

We do not expect to find such passages in contemporary Soviet literature—and they are still rare. But they have cropped up with increasing frequency in recent years. The authors feel constrained to assure their readers (and the authorities) that they are faithful atheists, but their depictions of believers and religious questions are increasingly sympathetic, or at least not hostile.

One senses a genuine spiritual quest by several Soviet writers who deal with religious themes. This trend predates the Gorbachev period by several years.

There has long been a debate among historians about whether history makes the individual or the individual makes history. In the case of Mikhail Gorbachev, *glasnost* did not spring full-grown out of one person's vision for the future. Rather it was a product of many factors, including the deteriorating economic situation, a general and undeniable moral crisis in the society, and a widespread readiness to consider more honestly the role past Soviet mistakes have played in the problems that fester today.

Literature is a good example of where the signs of *glasnost* can be detected before Gorbachev took power. Since the late1970s, there has been a more sympathetic treatment of religious believers in Soviet literature.

These encouraging breakthroughs, however, have had to occur in the teeth of the deathly legacy of "Socialist Realism." Dating to at least the First Congress of Soviet Writers (1934), Socialist Realism was an attempt to bring artistic method into conformity with ideological purpose. Reality was not to be described as it was but as it ought to be according to Communist theory. Emphasis was placed on finding meaning in service to the socialist community; little attention was given to the private lives of individuals. Any serious treatment of religious questions was avoided, except perhaps when describing an early stage in the "natural" evolution of individual views from the darkness of religious superstition toward the light of scientific materialism and atheism.

Although the World War II era produced a few good novels and short stories, Soviet literature since the 1930s has been a desert compared with the century before the October Revolution. The tsars had their censors, but Russian literature was nevertheless a gold mine of social commentary and creative religious thought. Not so since the time of Stalin. The best writers have been constantly hounded or silenced.

Ironically, but not untypically for Russia, at the very moment Socialist Realism was officially introduced, one of the most unusual and daring twentieth-century Russian novels was being composed—a bizarre fantasy in which the devil visits Moscow. Mikhail Bulgakov completed the *The Master and Margarita* just a few months before his own death in 1940. He knew it was impossible for his book to appear

in the Soviet Union in the foreseeable future. It was not until 1967-
1968 that *The Master and Margarita* finally appeared in a clumsily
edited Soviet edition.

Bulgakov does not write as a believer, but the book teems with
philosophical and theological discussions about Christ, Pilate, the
devil, and the nature of good and evil. At one point in the novel, Satan
ridicules a character for his one-dimensional or narrowly "materialist"
orientation:

> You spoke your words, as though you do not acknowledge
> the existence of shadows or of evil. Think now: where
> would your good be if there were no evil, and what would
> the earth look like without shadow? Shadows are thrown by
> people and things. There's the shadow of my sword. But
> shadows are also cast by trees and living beings. Do you
> want to strip the whole globe by removing every tree and
> everything alive to satisfy your fantasy of naked light? You
> are stupid.

In dealing with the poverty of atheist ideology, talk of the devil is as
scandalous and potentially corruptive as talk of God.

Eight years before Gorbachev came to power, Moscow's avant-
garde Taganka Theater premiered an adaptation of Bulgakov's novel.
I was in Moscow then, and the play was the talk of the town. It was
virtually impossible to get tickets, and there was a hushed awe in any
conversation when the play was mentioned.

For several months one of the world's great directors, Yury
Lyubimov, courageously continued the production. It was rumored
that some patron in the Kremlin was protecting Lyubimov, but
eventually the expected attack in *Pravda* occurred. Deciding that
Lyubimov could be tolerated no more, he was dismissed as director of
the Taganka Theater, expelled from the Communist party, and finally
stripped of his citizenship. One of the sure signs of *glasnost* is that
Lyubimov returned to direct two plays in the USSR during the
Gorbachev era, and in May 1989 his citizenship was restored. In
December 1989, he was once again named director of the Taganka
Theater.

If Soviet writers continue to insist that they are atheists, then how
does their writing reflect a positive change in their treatment of
religion? In the past, believers depicted in books or stories were
expected to conform to certain stereotypes. Priests frequently were

portrayed as drunkards living luxuriously off the gifts of their parishioners, and the suggestion of other moral problems was not unusual. The typical believer was invariably uneducated and superstitious. Believers were almost never productive members of society.

How different is the discussion of religion in the play *The Wood-Grouse's Nest* by Victor Rozov. The main character is the daughter of a leader in the Soviet peace movement. Her father comes home one day to their posh Moscow apartment and is shocked to find his daughter on her knees before his collection of icons. Her marriage in shambles, not even certain how to make the sign of the cross, she is praying: "Help me, God, help me."

Vladimir Tendriakov is another Soviet writer who explored moral and religious themes many years before Gorbachev came on the scene. His short stories from the late 1950s until his death in 1984 reflect a gradual but perceptible shift from the perspective of a typical atheist to someone with considerable respect for religious faith. His 1987 posthumously published novel *An Attack on Mirages* is filled with quotations from Scripture, commentary on Paul and Christ, and discussions about the relationship between science and religion.

Chingiz Aitmatov's *The Place of the Skull* is the novel with religious themes that has attracted the most attention in the Gorbachev period. Aitmatov is a popular writer from the Kirghiz Republic, and his own religious background is Moslem, though he is a professing atheist. His novel appeared in three parts in the journal *Novyi Mir* during 1986 and 1987.

The hero of the novel, Avdy Kallistratov, is on a spiritual quest to find a new religion which avoids both traditional Russian Orthodoxy and scientific materialism. He is also dedicated to turning people away from evil and toward a religion of love. Thrown off a train by drug dealers, he is eventually left to die suspended on a tree by thugs who are destroying the local wildlife. The parallels with the life of Christ are unmistakable.

Though the main character of The Place of the Skull is a moral, even religious, figure, he is by no means an orthodox Christian. He asserts that Judas fabricated the doctrines of the Resurrection and the Second Coming. The author expanded his own views on Jesus in a 1987 interview.

The legendary figure of Christ, which was very likely invented by men, is still a living figure to us today, one which teaches us a lofty and unforgettable lesson of personal courage and nobility. After Christ there were great men in all walks of life . . . but Jesus has outlived them all, appealing equally to men of the second and the twentieth centuries.

Publication of just the first third of Aitmatov's book provoked a frontal attack by the atheist establishment. In July 1986, I. Kryvelev, a senior Soviet authority on religion, launched the offensive against Aitmatov and two other Soviet writers (Astafev and Bykov) in the newspaper *Komsomol Pravda*. "To renounce a principled, consistent atheism," he contended, "is to renounce the very foundations of the scientific and materialistic world-view." The title of Kryvelev's article contained the heart of his critique: "Flirtation with a Dear Little God," an intentional reminder of Lenin's attack on "God-Seeking."

All that is at stake in the debate over religious themes in Soviet literature is not generally understood. On the most superficial level, a dogmatic atheist might object to any mention of religious themes in other than the most pejorative of forms. Religious themes at this level might represent either Christian orthodoxy or heresy. The crude atheist simply hears the word God and he sees red, never bothering to find out if the word is used in a sacred or heretical way.

(A distinction must be made between "God-Seeking" and "God-Building"—two early twentieth-century movements in Russia. Those considered "God-Seekers" were involved in a genuine move toward a traditional notion of a transcendent God, separate from humanity. In contrast, "God-Builders," recognizing the tremendous power religion has exercised in human history, wanted to harness religious language in the interests of a radically secular worship of humanity.)

It is premature to make a final judgment on Aitmatov's spiritual odyssey. Since he seems fascinated with Jesus Christ as a creative and powerful historical figure, it is possible he will come to understand Christ in a more orthodox and traditional manner.

It is important to separate the debate over the quality of the religious ideas being discussed in Soviet literature from the fact that there is discussion at all. It is encouraging, and indeed a sign of *glasnost*, that the dogmatic atheists' attack on Aitmatov was firmly met and turned back in the Soviet press by those who long for the fresh air of greater intellectual and cultural freedom.

The vigorous discussion in the Soviet press about the use of religious themes in literature is in itself a positive sign. Without question the positive treatment of religious figures and themes in Soviet literature is on the increase. It should not surprise us that these references to religion span the entire range from "God-Seeking" to "God-Building" and that many of them (such as allusions to the cultural vitality of the Old Believers and to beautiful churches) may reflect as much a revival of cultural nationalism as of revived religious consciousness.

However, as long as religious themes in Soviet literature can be discussed only by sympathetic atheists and not by committed believers, we have a long way to go before the spiritual and literary riches of the Soviet peoples can be mined in full. Yet in the literary circles there is an air of expectancy, a sense of the possibility of more fully entering into the broad, impressive stream of the cultures of the Soviet Union—cultures permeated with religious themes. Though steps in this direction are still tentative, they are nonetheless real.

REVIVAL OF RELIGIOUS ARCHITECTURE

One of my hobbies during my graduate studies in the Soviet Union was to track down and photograph old churches. Novgorod, in northeast Russia, is one of the Soviet Union's medieval gems. After considerable searching, I managed to locate, well off the beaten track, a twelfth-century church. But something was not quite right. There were flower boxes in the upstairs windows and electrical wires coming from the roof. Finally the awful truth sank in. This architectural masterpiece had been turned into an apartment building.

Actually this church was one of the lucky ones. Tens of thousands of others were razed or turned into warehouses, concert halls, or whatever else the local authorities deemed appropriate for advancing the social needs of the post-religious Communist community.

This desecration is tragic, and yet it is ironic that some of the best restoration work in Europe has been done in the Soviet Union. The golden onion domes, whitewashed exteriors, and exquisite interiors of many churches have found their way into countless thousands of tourist slide shows.

Unfortunately, many more churches were destroyed than preserved, and it is against that destruction that many have actively protested during the *glasnost* era. In 1986 esteemed academician Dmitry Likhachev (not to be confused with the conservative Kremlin ideologue Ligachev) established a Cultural Fund. The presidium of the organization includes Gorbachev's wife, Raisa, and Metropolitan Pitirim, head of the Moscow Patriarchate's publishing department.

The fund has raised millions of roubles to advance what Likhachev calls an "ecology of culture." He charges that Soviet culture is in a catastrophic state caused by moral nihilism. Before the Revolution, each church was a moral educator of the nation. In the wake of the destruction and massive closings of the churches, a moral vacuum remains where once were notions of good and evil, right and wrong.

A graphic literary example of the contemporary protest against the Soviet destruction of culture is found in a short story by Victor Astafev, published in the same year the Cultural Fund was set up. The author describes how invading Mongols in the fourteenth century set up camp in an ancient church. When they lit bonfires, lead in the dome of the church melted and poured down its molten judgment on the Mongols' heads. Reflecting on this scene, Astafev writes: "Oh, if only a heavenly rain of molten lead, that final and punishing rain, would fall on the heads of all desecrators of churches, of all haters of mankind, of all persecutors of pure morals."

Considerable attention has been given in the Western and Soviet press to the "generosity" of the state in returning to the Russian Orthodox church some of its most sacred and prized architectural treasures. In 1983 the Danilov Monastery in Moscow was given back to the church and has become an important new center for the Russian Orthodox Patriarchate. In 1987 the keys to the well-known Optina Monastery and the Yaroslavl Tolgsky Monastery were handed over to the church as well.

On the occasion of the 1987 returns, Alexander Nezhnyi, one of the most notable Soviet correspondents on religious matters, wrote a superb article on the historical, cultural, and religious significance of Optina. Nezhnyi reported that when the monastery was returned to its original owner, it looked like it had been bombed in an air raid. He estimated that fifteen million roubles would be needed to restore it, but he had no doubt that the faithful believers would raise that amount, just as they had come up with the necessary funds to restore the Danilov Monastery a few years before.

Nezhnyi also wrote an article on the Tolgsky Monastery. For six centuries the church lovingly maintained this architectural treasure, observed the correspondent, but after just sixty years in Soviet hands "the monastery presents a sorry sight . . . monks' cells are in ruin, doors and windows and their frames have disappeared . . . of the famous 160 giant cedars only twenty-seven have survived."

What is particularly remarkable about Nezhnyi's 1988 article is his appeal to all Soviet citizens, believers and nonbelievers alike, to give funds for the restoration of the church. A bank account number is provided so that contributors will know where to send their donations.

Soviet tourist guides are also being more honest about the fate of past architectural monuments. In the spring of 1988, our guide in Moscow showed us the site where Christ the Savior Cathedral had been dynamited in 1930 in order to construct a building. When the site would not support it, a large swimming pool was put in its place.

At the recent Seventh Writers' Congress, one of the Soviet Union's most famous poets, Andrei Voznesensky, reminded those present of what had happened to Christ the Savior Cathedral and noted that the building of that cathedral had been a truly "national" affair, in contrast to the indifference with which contemporary Soviet citizens greet the building of monuments. "This indifference disfigures our whole present," Voznesensky asserted.

It is impossible to miss the moral outrage that has emerged in recent months over the damage inflicted by the Communist authorities on these cultural treasures. Nor is it just the physical buildings that are being defended by many of those involved in the restoration movement. Likhachev has ridiculed atheist propaganda, calling it "ignorant . . . not only . . . of church history, but of history as a whole . . . ignorant of culture, [particularly] the culture of democracy." The "ecology of culture" movement is a strong force for religious freedom on the contemporary Soviet scene.

SOVIET FILMS

To a believer, there can be no spiritual *perestroika* apart from confession and repentance. While much of Soviet society is talking about a kind of *glasnost* which acknowledges economic and political shortcomings, there are others who are exploring much more profound depths of the human soul. One such person is Georgian film director Tengiz Abuladze. His movie *Repentance (Pokaiane)* is perhaps the most moving cultural event thus far in the Gorbachev era, though the conception of the project itself predates Gorbachev's rise to power.

Beginning like a bizarre surrealistic comedy, the film thrusts itself into the viewer's imagination. A small-town Georgian mayor,

Varlam Aravidze, has just been buried. However, his body keeps showing up in his relatives' backyard. We soon learn that an apparently crazy woman, Ketivan Barateli, is exhuming the body on a daily basis.

At her trial, it becomes obvious to the viewer that this is no ordinary comedy; it is a devastating attack on Georgian-born Joseph Stalin—the Mussolini/Hitler-like model for the deceased mayor. Ketivan's father, a Christlike artist, was one of Varlam's victims. The film contains graphic, emotional footage of family members seeking the names of loved ones carved into the ends of logs brought down from the forests. Indeed, this is how the victims of some of Stalin's forest gulags attempted to communicate with their wives and children.

Ketivan's sanity is questioned by the prosecution. After all, is it not both immoral and pointless to dig up the dead? But "Avaridze is not dead," exclaims the defendant. Moving in for the kill, the prosecutor pounces, "Then you believe he's alive?!" Ketivan fires back, "Yes he is! For as long as you continue to defend him, he lives on and continues to corrupt society."

But the movie is far more than an appeal to speak honestly about Stalin; it is a plea for spiritual soul searching. Undoubtedly the most moving lines of the movie are spoken at the end. In a flashback to the scene which opened the film, an old woman knocks on the window of the apartment where Ketivan is baking cakes.

> "Is this the road to the church?"
> Ketivan answers, "This is Varlam street. It will not take you to the church."
> "Then what's the use of it," the old woman replies. "What good is a road if it does not lead to a church?"

A more eloquent statement about the importance of both religious freedom and the spiritual dimension of life would be difficult to find in any country. That this powerful appeal for the spiritual dimension of life has been allowed to play to packed theaters in the largest cities of the Soviet Union is an unmistakable sign of glasnost.

The film sensation of 1990 was *One Shouldn't Live Like This* (*Tak Nelzia Zhit*). This graphic documentary of the moral squalor of contemporary Soviet society is the work of Stanislav Govorukhin, a gifted film producer of comedies.

Initially the film was banned by the censors, but through the direct intervention of the USSR Supreme Soviet, the ban was lifted in mid-1990 and the Soviet parliament was one of the first groups to see it. Gorbachev watched in silence, and then left looking grim. Passages from the film began to appear in speeches in the Supreme Soviet, and it is being seen by hundreds of thousands of people throughout the Soviet Union.

Govorukhin is not known to be a Christian, but his description of the problem is profoundly spiritual. In an interview about the film, Govorukhin asserts: "Society is immoral. There is no law, no morality, and it deserves to drown in crime. There is no God, no law. . . . A society without hope has to collapse."

While one film honestly examines the moral morass which is the legacy of over seventy years of communist rule, another is in preparation which may point a way out. In 1988, film director Mykola Machenko began working on the script for a movie on the life of Christ. The focus of the film, according to *Sovetskaia Kultura* (Soviet Culture), is on the sufferings and death sentence of Jesus. Filming began in 1990.

The stirrings of new life in Soviet literature and in the cultural revival may have at first represented phenomena which were being allowed by the regime for its own purposes. Nonetheless they also represent a genuine and significant new spirit of religious interest in the Soviet Union.

CHAPTER 5

RELIGION IN
THE PUBLIC SQUARE:
STEPS TOWARD PLURALISM

*M*any in the West have long asserted that religion is alive and well in the Soviet Union, and it is true that religion has survived and much of it is vibrant. There is also considerable evidence in recent years of a growing interest in religion among the Soviet population, including the well-educated.

But the impact of more than seventy years of militantly antireligious propaganda has taken its toll. In my living in and travel to the Soviet Union, I have often talked to intelligent and well-educated Soviet citizens who have never been exposed to a positive view of religion; it invariably has been presented as fundamentally superstitious and antiscientific. To be sure, they knew there was some persecution and that not everything the government said about believers was true. But the lack of an opportunity to hear intelligent Christians describe and defend their beliefs had deprived these nonreligious Soviets of even a rudimentary knowledge of basic Christian beliefs.

Our Intourist guide during a two-week Millennium Tour in 1988 illustrated this problem well. The idea that an educated person could seriously consider religious belief, let alone be a believer, was not something she had ever thought possible.

The official Soviet line on church/state matters has moderated. There is a greater willingness to acknowledge past "mistakes" by the government, to explore the possibility of believers contributing positively to the common good, and to support the release of prisoners of conscience. Religion has long represented what any authoritarian or totalitarian state fears most—a competing source of ultimate allegiance. However, by the early 1990s, the Kremlin seems genuinely uninterested in pursuing its historical animosity toward believers.

Before any more definitive judgments are proposed, we must supplement fragmentary firsthand interviews with a careful analysis of how religion is faring in the Soviet press.

RELIGION AND THE SOVIET PRESS

In November 1986, Mikhail Gorbachev, demanded a "decisive and uncompromising struggle against manifestations of religion and a strengthening of political work with the masses and of religious propaganda."

Just seventeen months later, in late April 1988, Gorbachev sounded remarkably more tolerant about the positive role of believers in Soviet society. During a reception at the Kremlin for the top leadership of the Russian Orthodox church, he told a nationwide television audience, "Believers are Soviet people, workers, patriots, and they have the full right to express their conviction with dignity. *Perestroika* and democratization concern them too—in full measure and without any restrictions."

How do we account for these apparently contradictory attitudes? A Soviet spokesman passed off Gorbachev's November 1986 comment as "just for party members." But there seems to have been a deliberate and remarkable change in Soviet policy sometime between late 1986 and 1987.

There is strong evidence that a crude and typically negative treatment of believers in the Soviet press lasted at least until the end of 1986. It appears that Gorbachev's November 1986 comment came near the end of one last offensive initiated by the hard-line antireligious ideologues. One of the clearest signs of the lack of *glasnost* in the mid-1980s was the hysterical denunciations of Keston College (England), the foremost research center for the study of religion in Communist countries. The 1985 booklet *Argumenty 85*, with a press run of 150,000, accused Keston College general director Michael Bourdeaux of having connections with the CIA and of "fabricating and juggling the facts" to perpetuate the "dying myth" of "persecuted believers" in the Soviet Union. A few months later, the Soviets would publish materials that supported what Bourdeaux and

Keston had been saying for years. Leningrad TV even interviewed Bourdeaux when he visited the Soviet Union in 1988—his first trip into the country in nine years!

The 27th Party Congress in Moscow in February 1986 depicted religion as old-fashioned, reactionary, and tied up with dangerous nationalist tendencies. Well into 1986 both national and local newspapers contained numerous attacks on believers of all denominations. Typical of these crude attacks is the June 1986 article in *Science and Religion*, which pictures the God of the Old Testament as a vengeful, bloodthirsty spirit. In short, the data is strong that at least until late 1986, the treatment of believers and religion in the Soviet press was "business as usual."

By the fall of 1987, however, change was in the wind. In Keston College's Annual Report (September 1987), the following assessment appeared:

> Anti-religious articles continue to be regularly published, but it is no longer taboo for Pravda to admit that religion is not only surviving but attracting new members, particularly among young people. The interest shown in religious themes and Christian ethics by leading writers such as Aitmatov and Rasputin is certainly criticized but is nevertheless discussed in some detail.

One of the most promising signs of change is the occasional defense of believers in the local press when they are the victims of vicious slander. In 1987 Father Nikolai Sakidon, a thirty-three-year-old priest from near Kharkov in Ukraine was assaulted in the press (*October Dawn*) by local authorities who were zealous atheists. The matter came to the attention of Sergei Kiselev, a press correspondent, who then published an interview with the priest in the well-known national magazine *Literary Gazette*.

The article is positive toward the young priest, who is credited with significantly increasing the giving at his church. He is warmly praised by his archbishop as "an honest and conscientious pastor . . . held in great respect by the clergy and by believers." Even Communist authorities are quoted as opposing the slander campaign conducted against him. N. Kolesnik, chairman of the Ukrainian Council for Religious Affairs, the government watchdog committee over religion, notes that slanderous articles reduce believers to "second-class" citizens and violate government regulations of atheist propaganda.

A remarkable article appeared in *Leningrad Pravda* (March 22, 1988). The article was called "Is It Possible to Forbid Attending Church? *Perestroika* and Religion," and would have been unheard of ten years ago. The author, A. Ignatov, attacks local authorities for not knowing well the legislation dealing with religion. He reminds his readers that believers have the legal right to profess any religion and carry out the rites associated with it. Yet letters to the paper and his own investigations have confirmed that local authorities frequently harass believers.

A prominent example that Ignatov cites is the attempt to destroy churches. He tells of a letter from twelve Russian Orthodox believers from the Ukrainian village of Ilemnia reporting that their church was "temporarily" closed in 1961 and never reopened. In addition, for almost three years now they have had to protect the church from destruction. The letter went on to assert that in July 1985 the local authorities closed a church in the village of Luga and intended to tear it down. Only the believers' willingness to stand guard around the closed church prevented its demolition. However, the believers were fined, summoned before the authorities, and pressured to attend churches in other villages. Ignatov bristles: "What gives regional administrators the right to determine where citizens may or may not go to church?"

The Soviet journalist is not satisfied with listing a few examples of local administrative malfeasance. He documents that between 1962 and 1987 almost no new churches were opened, while many were closed. Ignatov observes: "It is no secret that official channels consider that 'religious prejudices ought to quickly die out' and that's why church buildings are not needed."

Ignatov charges that the local authorities view believers with suspicion. They see them as ideological enemies. "And this is what is paradoxical. We are learning how to converse in a normal human language with a real ideological enemy from the West, but with our own citizens—born and raised under socialism—we do not always follow the same humane laws." And it's not just local authorities who are heavy-handed. Ignatov scolds teachers who insensitively quiz the children of believers on why they believe in God.

But Ignatov is optimistic, though he admits the process of improving attitudes toward believers is slow. He cites as hopeful signs the increase in the output of religious literature and the return of important monasteries and churches to ecclesiastical control.

According to the journalist, a similar change is occurring in government attitudes toward other religions as well as toward Christianity; it is not just a matter of the millennium celebrations scheduled for June.

Many articles in the Soviet press in subsequent months followed a similar pattern. The following problems were typically acknowledged: violation of laws or regulations, as well as arbitrary behavior, by local authorities; destruction of churches; serious delays or obstacles created by local authorities in registering churches; and rude, unfair treatment of believers by propagandists or teachers. The positive traits of believers were also more likely to be noted than in the past.

Not infrequently, officials connected with propaganda are involved in strong self-criticism. In the November 1988 issue of *Religion and Science,* A. G. Khmyrchik, the head of the propaganda section for the Kaliningrad Oblast (Province), asserts that the propaganda stereotypes of the church are breaking down. Vulgar criticism of believers is likely to evoke a strong reaction from both believers and nonbelievers. We have come a long way when the following can be published in an official Soviet journal:

> The time has come to put an end forever to suspicious and hostile attitudes to believers and to such ideals cherished by them as humanism, love, moral self-improvement. . . . The existence of millions of believers . . . is not an unfortunate error of history, but a reality. . . . The church has succeeded in finding a place for herself in the socialist society without waiving her teachings, without deceiving either the believers or the state.

The author does not reject atheism itself but rather the crude, intolerant form it has sometimes taken. The challenge is issued for atheism to appeal to the same inner instincts which draw people to religious belief.

In the quest to explain the resilience, and even growth, of religion, Soviet scholars have shown some willingness to note the role socialism's shortcomings may have played. Dr. Alexander Klibanov of the USSR Academy of Sciences' Institute of USSR History connects the growth of religious communities to the failure of socialism to live up to its ideals. What is missing, of course, is any recognition that an individual's religious inclinations may be positive and innate rather than an escape from deficiencies in the social environment.

One of toughest *glasnost* barriers to breech is the one forbidding criticism of Lenin. Ever since 1970, when Russian emigres published a "Top Secret" 1922 letter from Lenin, Soviet authorities have insisted that the letter was a forgery. The letter explodes the myth that Lenin never attacked the church in a deliberately cruel and cynical manner. Lenin demands that the famine be used as a pretext to expropriate church valuables, that extreme cruelty be used so that it will be remembered for decades, and that the money be used in part to build up the Red Army (and thus not for famine relief). The letter has now been published by both *Sobesednik* (Conversationist) and by the Communist party's Central Committee newspaper.

The television coverage and the dozens of articles in the Soviet press that have been more positive toward religion in recent years have evoked a strong reaction in certain quarters. In April 1989, a professor of Marxist-Leninism wrote an angry denunciation of what he considered the "pro-religion" bias of the press. He charges that the positive treatment of believers in the press amounts to allowing them to propagate their views, and thus violates Article 52 of the Constitution which gives only atheists the right to propound their views in public. He contends that when children were taken by the state from religious families it was not because of their faith, but because they violated the laws. This professor is distressed that in all of 1988, apart from the articles which appeared in *Science and Religion*, only two atheist articles came out (one in *Kommunist* and one in *Pravda*), and this is in clear violation of the 1988 Central Committee resolution calling for increased "attention to atheistic education."

The same issue of the journal contains a response by another scholar who says it is true that " 'Atheism' has not simply gone out of style, it has almost become a dirty word." But he defends all the attention to religion in the press and notes that the "blank spots" of their country "ooze with the color of blood." The lesson here is that though militant atheists are on the defensive, they are not yet vanquished and they are disturbed by the course of contemporary events.

Meanwhile, the more positive treatment of believers in the media shows no signs of letting up. Historian Valery Lebedev and journalist Tatiana Cherniaeva are collaborating on a series of films on Christians and religion in the Soviet Union. In May 1990, I was shown a draft text of the first film, and it was very moving. The prologue asserts that millions of religious believers of all faiths had been persecuted by Soviet totalitarianism and that the purpose of these films was to tell about their fates.

> But the story of these tragic fates is not just one of trial and ordeal. It is a story about overcoming these trials. It is the story of a real accomplishment in opposition to totalitarianism. Stalin's reign killed tens of millions of the people of Russia. It attempted to crucify the conscience and soul of the people. But the people did not perish. The believers of Russia completed their journey, their journey to the cross, ascending a twentieth-century Golgotha. With their painful fortunes they proved the ineradicability of faith.

This kind of public narrative represents something far more profound than shedding the earlier negative treatment of religion; it represents a quest for religious roots, and it is cropping up more and more often in the media.

CHRISTIANS GAIN ACCESS TO MASS MEDIA

It is one thing to receive more favorable treatment at the hands of a mainly atheist or secular press, and quite another to have one's own direct access to the public through the media.

As of August 1, 1990, a new law on the press and mass media went into effect which guarantees to religious groups, as to state and public organizations, the right to set up their own publications (Article 7). Depending on who the publication addresses and its size, it will have to be registered with either the republic or the Union authorities. Registration must be granted unless the publication jeopardizes state security; calls for a violent overthrow of the system; expresses racial, national, or religious intolerance; promotes warmongering; or is pornographic (Article 5).

If this law is implemented, and if the "state security" concerns are not interpreted as in the past (that is, religion undermines the social fabric of the country and plays into the hands of the USSR's foreign enemies), then this will represent an important breakthrough for Christians and members of other religious groups. Since this new press law is in conflict with Article 52 of the USSR Constitution, which guarantees to atheists alone the right to propagate their views in public, Article 52 will need to be amended if the new law is to function as it ought.

Another breakthrough occurred on June 15, 1990, when Trans World Radio (TWR) dedicated a recording studio in Leningrad. Located in the bell tower of a former Orthodox church given to the Baptists by the authorities in 1989, the studio will be used to record interviews, testimonies, music, and discussions for later broadcast. There are plans for TWR to set up studios in Moscow, Minsk, and Brest.

Trans World Radio has years of experience and knowledge in dealing with the Soviet religious scene. Unfortunately, the same is not true for some Western evangelical organizations which may seek ministry opportunities in the Soviet Union. Their limited knowledge of the Soviet scene will make it extremely difficult for them to be as sensitive as they ought to be to the culture, particularly its Orthodox history. A negative encounter or two will do great damage to the possibility of responsible Western ministry among the peoples of the USSR.

In the spring of 1986 International Russian Radio/TV received from the Christian Broadcasting Network (CBN) the Russian rights to a children's video series titled "Superbook." By the spring of 1988 the first videos of this highly successful animated Bible series were brought into the Soviet Union. A year later, during the filming of a Soviet television documentary in Leningrad on Christian activity in the USSR, the "Superbook" video being watched by some of the children caught the attention of the filmmakers and a portion of the video was played in the documentary. By late September Leningrad Television (25 million viewing audience) broadcast an entire episode of "Superbook," and in December a Christmas episode was broadcast over the Latvian (2.5 million) and Estonian (1.5 million) television networks. The broadcasts gave the address of IRR and thousands of letters from Soviet citizens poured into Finland. These letters, the interest of a correspondent from *Izvestiia*, and the enthusiastic support of the Ministry of Health eventually led to negotiations for opening a ministry center near Moscow.

A major breakthrough came on April 20, 1990, when Soviet Central Television (Moscow), with an audience of over 200 million people in all fifteen republics, signed an agreement to air "Superbook" beginning in late May. Each segment was scheduled to air four times and the contract is operative through May 1991. This television presentation of the gospel to millions of Soviet citizens is unprecedented.

Beginning in September 1990, International Russian Radio/TV began broadcasting its own evangelism program on Soviet television to seventy million viewers in twenty-seven regions. Even more amazing, in early 1991, it was scheduled to begin airing on all twenty-five hundred Soviet radio stations its weekly evangelism program. According to the agreement, permission exists to broadcast the addresses of five counseling centers which have been set up in the USSR. As the chairman for Soviet National radio put it in the fall of 1990: "We are giving you our maximum, the total capacity of our whole network."

RELIGION IN THE PUBLIC SCHOOLS

Today, as a consequence of an atheistic upbringing, we are knee-deep in alcoholics, drug addicts, other chemically-dependent individuals, loafers, bums, criminals, savages, uncouths, dullards, cruel and frightful juveniles who commit crimes for the fun of it. These are people who were brought up by non-believer parents and an atheistic society. Christians lived with religion for 1,000 years and provided us with a rich heritage, which we have succeeded in destroying without fire or flood. . . . It would be a very good thing if, in restructuring the school curriculum, the education specialists included teaching of religion in our schools.

The angry woman in Kiev who wrote the above letter may not be versed in the fine points of church/state separation as debated in the U.S., but she is convinced that she sees a connection between atheist education and a society without moral moorings. Many in the Soviet Union, including educated sociologists, believe she is right. Of course, alcoholism existed in Russia under the tsars, and all of these problems exist in the West where there is religious freedom today, but her basic contention has to do with whether religion ought to be taught in the public schools. Incidentally, there are critics in the West who argue that these same problems in part exist in the West precisely because many children receive little or no moral or religious training either at home or at school.

Just a few years ago believers in the Soviet Union were

imprisoned for simply trying to set up private religious education for their children. Before a new law came into existence formally allowing religious organizations to set up their own educational facilities, the public schools opened up to some religious instruction on a voluntary basis, or at least to more serious study about religion. The new law neither explicitly allows nor forbids the use of public school facilities for voluntary religious instruction.

The Baltic states have led the way, however, in allowing religious instruction. Tass reported in the fall of 1988 that a Lutheran pastor would begin teaching a course in the history of religion in some Riga schools. In February 1990, it was reported that Riga University had established a theological faculty. The students for this faculty will be believers, and the teachers will include Protestant, Catholic, and Russian Orthodox theologians. By at least 1989 Lithuania was offering courses in religion. An agreement between the Lithuanian Committee for Public Education and Cardinal Sladkevicius of the Catholic Bishops Conference now allows the teaching of the Bible in the classroom. The parents or guardians decide on whether their child will attend and the Bishops Conference provides the instructors. In Estonia, under the rubric of "cultural history," some priests have been brought on as teachers.

Early in 1990 Vazgen I, the Supreme Patriarch and Catholicos of the Armenian Apostolic church, gave the first lecture in a new course, "The Bible as a Monument of World Culture." Yerevan Pedagogical Institute was not used to such lectures, but the new offering is part of a new part of the curriculum: "The History and Theory of Religion and Atheism." It replaces a course in scientific atheism, which was said not to "meet the needs of the present day." The Echmiadzin Theological Seminary is helping to organize the course.

The progressive democratic forces presently in leadership positions in the RFSFR Supreme Soviet are aware of the difference between teaching about religion and teaching religion. In 1990, they passed legislation which makes mandatory a course on monotheism (Judaic, Christian, and Islamic) on the assumption that no educated person can be ignorant about these religions. In addition, they are working on providing elective classes which openly teach theology. In order to avoid returning to the tsarist days of an "established religion," parents of the school children in question would have to approve their children attending catechism or theology classes.

There are those within the hierarchy of the Russian Orthodox church who favor simply replacing "atheism" with "Russian Orthodoxy" as the favored state ideology. Some members of the hierarchy approached an important Soviet official with precisely that suggestion.

Some in the Orthodox church, however, and many representatives of other religious groups are interested in Western models which proscribe any "established" religious group, and which guarantee freedom of conscience for all peoples—believers and nonbelievers alike. And yet, there may be more openness in the Soviet Union in some circles (including some nonbeliever circles) today to providing elective religion classes in public schools than there is even in the U.S. An article in an April 1990 issue of *Literaturnaia Gazeta* asserts that it is now time for youth to choose their own beliefs. This is what the teachers of School No. 1100 in Moscow believe and it is why they organized a club at the school to study the Russian Orthodox church and Orthodox culture. An Orthodox priest comes each Friday to show a religious film, give a talk, or discuss the Bible with students and parents. Keston College reports that priests are being invited into many schools during the *glasnost* era.

CONCLUSION

There are some who are still concerned that the Kremlin is trying to co-opt the church by liberalizing government policy toward it. If this is what the Soviets are up to, then they are playing a dangerous game, for the increased freedoms now enjoyed by the churches provide them with greatly enhanced opportunities to expand their influence. The fruits of these opportunities may well overwhelm a cynical, atheist government's attempt to control them.

Only time will tell. The stakes are high for both the government and for Christians. Western observers will need to monitor the situation carefully if they expect to be in a position to help their co-believers in the Soviet Union.

CHAPTER 6

THE IMPACT OF *GLASNOST* ON CHRISTIAN BELIEVERS
PART I

*T*he Soviet Union in the Mikhail Gorbachev era is a kaleidoscope of contradictory and competing realities.

There are many signs of a liberalized policy towards believers: releases from labor camp, more positive treatment of religion in the press, Christian access to the mass media, major admission of past government violation of religious freedoms, increased scope of activities allowed to believers, and permission to import or print large quantities of religious literature. There are also continuing problems, which must not be ignored.

No one should expect that the damage done in three quarters of a century can be undone overnight. Nor can patterns of discrimination simply be decreed out of existence. Furthermore, the debate is only in its early stages as to what role religion can or ought to play in Soviet society. But change has definitely come, and in many important ways Christians have benefited from developments in what has been called "religious *perestroika*."

RELEASE OF RELIGIOUS PRISONERS

An unmistakable sign of *glasnost* has been the steady decline in the number of religious and political prisoners. From March 1985, when Gorbachev took over, to May 25, 1988, the number of Christian prisoners dropped by more than 300 to 19, while the number of religious prisoners overall was reduced from about 420 to 73.

Among those Christians released from labor camp or exile was

Nikolai Boiko. Pastor Boiko had been away from his Odessa Baptist congregation for more than eight years when finally he was allowed to return from eastern Siberia. Unregistered pastors from throughout the country traveled to southern Ukraine for the long-awaited reunion. The service lasted several hours, there were many sermons and testimonies, and much singing. The theme of the day was taken from Christ's words: "I will build my church, and the gates of hell shall not prevail against it."

Finally the moment came for Boiko to address the gathering. He told of being reared in a family of nonbelievers, drafted into the Soviet Army, captured by the Nazis and taken to the Buchenwald concentration camp. On a work detail in Berlin he encountered the Lord's Prayer through a Polish prisoner. Eventually, belief in God was born and he began to pray.

Like many Soviet soldiers captured by the Nazis, upon his repatriation to the Soviet Union, Stalin sent him to Siberia as a "spy." It was in the far north that he became a dedicated Christian, and he was formally baptized in 1953 upon his release from labor camp.

He was arrested in 1968 after his church refused to register with the authorities. Four terms and twenty years later, having survived the deprivations and loneliness of labor camp and exile, Boiko testified to the faithfulness of God, as did his wife who stood with him through it all. Such is but one of the human faces behind the decline in the number of Christians in prison, labor camp, or exile. There are many such stories.

Fewer Christians in Psychiatric Hospitals

Internment in Soviet mental institutions has been one of the most vicious forms of persecution endured by prisoners of conscience. Many fully sane Christians have been subjected to drugs and indefinite confinement in an effort to break their spirits, and if necessary, their minds and bodies.

In the 1960s, but even more in the 1970s, the Soviets used psychiatric hospitals as confinement facilities. Medical authorities there reported directly to the Ministry of Interior. Andrei Snezhevsky invented the term "sluggish schizophrenia" to describe those dissidents in the Brezhnev era who possessed "an excessive desire for social justice." In 1981, Dr. Anatoly Koryagin was sent to labor camp for refusing to diagnose a healthy dissident as insane, and for protesting against the abuse of psychiatry.

In 1988 the "special" psychiatric hospitals were transferred from the Ministry of Interior to the Ministry of Health. And the Soviets themselves have begun to acknowledge abuses. Psychiatrist Mikhail Buyanov wrote an article for a Soviet publication in 1981 in which he praised Koryagin for exposing the abuse of psychiatry in the USSR. (In 1987 Koryagin was allowed to emigrate, and as late as November 1988 he contended that there were still sane dissidents in Soviet mental institutions.)

Early in 1989 a delegation of American psychiatrists was allowed to travel to the Soviet Union and examine present and past psychiatric patients. Their report released in July was sobering. Based on their findings and other persistent reports of continuing problems, Rep. Steny H. Hoyer, cochairman of the U.S. Commission on Security and Cooperation in Europe, said "neither *glasnost* nor *perestroika* has yet had the impact on Soviet psychiatry that we have observed in other aspects of Soviet life."

Particularly troubling to human rights advocates in the West has been the Kremlin failure to remove from prime leadership spots in Soviet psychiatry the very individuals who presided over the worst abuses of the past. Another issue which has upset human rights observers is the deplorable conditions within the mental institutions. As Peter Reddaway has put it, "The current situation in Soviet psychiatry needs a surrealist of Kafka's skill to describe it."

The lingering problems in Soviet psychiatry continue to have some impact on the Christian community. In August 1990, Keston College identified two Baptists who still may be in psychiatric hospitals, though neither appears to be in prison for specifically religious reasons. Anatoly Matvienko was first consigned to a psychiatric institution in 1985, but managed to escape. He was in trouble for criticizing the government. Recaptured, he was sentenced to eight years in a strict regime labor camp. He often found himself in trouble for protesting against the treatment of prisoners by the camp administration and for supporting Andrei Sakharov's December 1989 call for a political strike. Twice he was sent to a psychiatric hospital. During the Gorbachev era, he has been badly beaten, and in May 1990 he was taken from a labor camp to an unknown destination. It is not known whether he is in another camp or back in a psychiatric institution.

Vladimir Novikov was arrested in 1983 at age seventeen for painting anti-party slogans on the walls of the Voronezh city council.

Interned in a psychiatric hospital, he escaped, was taken in by Baptists, but has been rearrested and sent to the Volgograd Special Psychiatric Hospital. He has become a Christian, but the staff of the "hospital" consider his evangelistic letters to friends as a manifestation of his socially dangerous illness.

THE SLANDER OF BELIEVERS LESSENS

In spite of marked improvement in the treatment of believers in the press, there are still graphic signs that the politics of government slander and intimidation have been utilized in the Gorbachev era.

The state's venom has been particularly aimed at Alexander Ogorodnikov, one of the leading Russian Orthodox dissidents. Reasons for the state's ire against Ogorodnikov are not hard to come by. As a well-educated former Marxist committed to spreading the faith, he is an ever-present reminder of the failure of the official Soviet ideology to inspire and hold on to its young. In 1974, at the age of thirty-four, Ogorodnikov and his friend Vladimir Poresh founded the Christian Seminar. Deliberately emulating earlier religio-philosophical circles of the pre-Revolutionary period, intellectuals from several major Soviet cities formed a nucleus of spiritual vitality—a vitality new converts often could not find in the timid official church with its severely restrained religious activities.

The intimidation and persecution of Christian Seminar members was fierce beginning in 1976. They lost their jobs, were subjected to surveillance and arbitrary searches, and were sent to labor camp. Ogorodnikov was arrested and condemned to labor camp in 1978 for parasitism, anti-Soviet agitation, and propaganda. He suffered greatly while in confinement, deprived of what he treasured most on this earth: the opportunity to read and write. He had an indomitable will and at one point maintained a modified hunger strike for two years. He was finally released in 1987.

It has long been Soviet policy to coerce religious figures to recant. This was still going on in 1986. In April of that year, Boris Razveyev, a Russian Orthodox church member of the Christian Seminar (earlier imprisoned for participating in private religious discussion groups and one of Ogorodnikov's friends) denounced his own "anti-Soviet" behavior and made the absurd charge that Ogorodnikov was a rapist and a sexual pervert. The slander was later repeated on national television. The KGB had circulated these allegations since Ogorodnikov's first arrest in 1978. This sort of public slander continued several years into *glasnost*.

The Soviet press in the Gorbachev era has slandered unregistered religious groups. In September 1986 Pentecostal leaders were charged with "holding children in a deadly grip" and "adding narcotic substances to believers' food." Unregistered Baptists who were on trial in March 1987 were pilloried by the press as "ringleaders of schismatics," "obscurantists," and "parasites."

Believers are grateful, however, that the slander seems to be lessening, and not to have been present to any significant degree in 1989 and 1990.

A NEW SEMI-OPENNESS TO FOREIGN CRITICS

One of the most tangible evidences of glasnost has been Soviet willingness to grant visas to those who have publicized the repression of religion in the USSR. Michael Bourdeaux, general director of Keston College, was permitted three visits to the Soviet Union between June 1988 and September 1990. Even more unusual was the invitation from the Soviet Novosti Press Agency for Bourdeaux to select a delegation of four associates of Keston College to come to the Soviet Union in April 1989 to discuss religious freedom and meet with government and religious figures. Unfortunately, just a few days before the trip, Novosti informed Keston that the trip had to be postponed for reasons beyond its control.

That foreign critics, pilloried in the past as "anti-Soviet" because they documented religious repression in the Soviet Union, have been granted visas is firm evidence of considerable change. Yet Soviet response to foreign critics is highly unpredictable, even contradictory. For example, in 1988 Bourdeaux picked up a brochure in English in Kiev's airport titled: "Prisoners of Conscience in the USSR and their Patrons." Published in 1988, the work slandered Keston College in a way as bad as or worse than anything the Soviets had ever written. Keston College was charged with being involved since its founding in espionage with the CIA. At his next meeting with a Novosti Press official, Bourdeaux asked how it was possible that he could be invited to participate in meetings with the Soviets at the very moment he was being slandered in print. The response: "The slander is a relic of the past. The brochure may have been published this year, but we will get rid of it."

The unpredictable character of Soviet reality once again imposed itself as Bourdeaux was rejected for visas in both August and October

1989. On the second occasion, he was the only person out of an eleven-person British Foreign Office Human Rights delegation who was refused. The British canceled the trip in protest. Allegedly, Bourdeaux had violated his February 1989 visa by going to Vilnius; in fact, he had been officially invited by the Bishop of Vilnius to visit and his visa approved the visit. But in early September 1990, Bourdeaux was allowed to attend a human rights conference in Leningrad, and there was no problem in receiving his visa.

After fourteen years of being denied visas, Peter and Anita Deyneka of the Slavic Gospel Association were allowed to travel to the Soviet Union in March 1989 and have returned several times since. They have had many productive meetings with evangelical Christians and discussed with government officials how Western Christians might help meet the religious literature and theological training needs of Soviet believers, as well as contribute to the resolution of a wide variety of societal and family problems.

Why have some foreign critics finally been allowed more freely into the Soviet Union? One reason seems apparent. The positive reports of previous critics mean more than the words of witnesses who consistently exaggerated the amount of religious freedom during the pre-Gorbachev era. It is a risky venture, however—if the liberalization begins to unravel, authorities will have a big problem hiding that fact from experienced observers.

SHOWCASING THE MILLENNIUM

It is always an awkward moment when openly atheist Communist leaders must decide what to do about a commemorative occasion involving a nation's religious heritage. Nineteen eighty-eight marked the one-thousand-year anniversary of the formal baptism in Kiev of the Eastern Slavs into Byzantine Christianity. The religious influence of Byzantine Christianity on the history of Russia and Ukraine is incalculable. There can be no adequate understanding of the history of Russia and Ukraine apart from a firm grasp of the importance of Christianity in shaping the culture of the empire's Slavic peoples.

For more than seventy years Communist antireligious propagandists had sought to exorcise Soviet citizens of their "reactionary" religious ideas. What sense did it make to celebrate the coming of Christianity to the medieval Slavic state? And besides, this celebration was fraught with difficulties. Ukrainian nationalists might try to use the occasion to highlight their own frustration at being absorbed into a larger, Russian-dominated Soviet empire.

Five years before Gorbachev took power, a government decision was made to commemorate the millennium; the state and the Russian Orthodox church would play leading roles. There can be little question that the Soviets were interested in damage control: "Better we be involved in organizing the celebration on our terms than genuinely independent religious groups on theirs." Still, what took place in 1988 represented important breakthroughs for religion in the Soviet Union.

Even before the formal events in June and July 1988, the Soviet media, beginning in March 1987, adopted a much more positive stance toward the church. A series of favorable articles appeared in the Soviet press in the months preceding and during millennium activities.

Another way in which *glasnost* positively affected the church during the millennium year was the April 29 meeting at the Kremlin between Russian Orthodox leaders and Mikhail Gorbachev. It had been more than forty years since such a meeting had occurred. *Izvestiia* gave front-page coverage to the event and quoted Gorbachev's reference to the millennium as "a significant milestone" in the country's history and culture. Furthermore, he referred to Christians in the USSR as "Soviet people, working people, patriots," and reported that the legislation on religion was being revised.

The main festivities were impressive. A special June 10 millennium commemorative concert at the Bolshoi Theater was attended by Raisa Gorbachev and then President Gromyko. Two days later a Divine Liturgy was held for ten thousand people in the square in front of the Danilov Monastery Cathedral. Special events were also held in Kiev, Vladimir, Leningrad, and other cities within the USSR. In all, more than fifteen hundred official guests attended various celebrations.

Millennium events, despite their limitations and state attempts to control the agenda, reflected a new, more positive attitude toward the Christian community. Millions of Soviets became aware of the religious significance of the occasion, and though there were some negative articles in the press, many were positive. Ten years before, who could have imagined such celebrations?

AT LAST: NEW LEGISLATION ON RELIGION

For decades the Soviet position was that full religious freedom was guaranteed by the Constitution and the laws of the USSR. This line was persistently maintained by registered Soviet church leaders in dealing with their Western co-religionists, and in a distressing number of cases the tale was repeated to millions of Western Christians by their own leaders.

But the facts were quite different. In a 1989 interview, Konstantin Kharchev, the Soviet Union's senior official then in charge of religious matters, was asked, "After sixty years, what is changing for religion in the country which is officially godless?" Kharchev responded: "The main thing is that believers of any faith will no longer be second-class citizens." Kharchev went on to assert that the "constitutional discrimination between atheists and believers must end." Although Kharchev claimed that efforts toward new religious legislation began in 1979, he said work "in earnest" began only around the beginning of 1986.

Registered religious organizations had some input into the proposed Law on Freedom of Conscience. The Council for Religious Affairs at the end of 1988 established a scientific-consultative commission, which included both religious figures and academic scholars, to discuss a CRA draft of the new legislation.

On May 30, 1990, a revision of the CRA draft Law on the Freedom of Conscience and Religious Organizations was given a first reading by the USSR Supreme Soviet. On June 5, it was published in *Izvestiia*. The government then presented proposals and comments from the public to the commission which had been drafting the law.

On October 1, 1990, the Law on Freedom of Conscience was passed by the USSR Supreme Soviet by a vote of 341 to 1, with one abstention. The draft which was finally approved reportedly reflected the suggestions or comments of fifteen hundred persons who responded to the call to respond to the draft published in *Izvestiia* in June. The law formally went into effect on October 9, when it was published in Pravda. Among the thirty-one articles are the following key provisions.

State-funded Atheist Teaching Abolished (Article 5). "The state does not fund religious organizations or activity associated with the propaganda of atheism." Though buried within Article 5, in many ways this is the most stunning clause in the new law. Formerly, not only was religion relentlessly attacked, but the public schools aggressively propagated the only perspective allowed—atheism. If this provision is fully implemented, Marxism as the official ideology of the government is dead. Nor, it must be noted, may the state fund religious organizations or activity.

The Right to Practice and Propagate Religious Beliefs (Articles 1, 5, 21). The first line of Article 1 states: "This law guarantees the rights of citizens to decide and express their attitude toward religion, to convictions corresponding to this, and to the unhindered confession of a religion and the exercise of religious rites." The right to disseminate religious views or evangelize is thus guaranteed.

Article 21 gives religious organizations "the right to found and maintain freely accessible places for divine service or religious gatherings." Services may be held in "prayer buildings . . . at places of pilgrimage, in the establishments of religious organizations, at cemeteries and crematoriums, and in citizen's apartments and houses." In addition, services may be conducted in "infirmaries, hospitals, homes for the aged and disabled, and in places of preliminary detention, and places where sentences are served . . . at the request of the citizens in them."

Right to Religious Literature (Articles 19, 22). Article 22 states: "Citizens and religious organizations have the right to acquire and make use of religious literature in the language of their choice." They may "produce, export, import, and disseminate" religious literature, as well as set up publishing establishments.

Right for Parents to Provide Children with a Religious Upbringing (Article 3). "Parents and persons acting *in loco parentis* have the right in mutual agreement to rear their own children in accordance with their personal attitudes toward religion."

Right to Religious Schooling (Articles 6, 11). Registered religious organizations have the right "to set up educational establishments and groups for the religious education of children and adults, and also to engage in teaching in other forms, making use of premises that they own or that are made available for their use for this" (Article 6). This provision allows for private religious education, and it does not rule out the possibility of the use of public school facilities for religious instruction. Article 11 allows religious groups to set up educational "establishments to train clergy and other ministers."

Equal Rights for All Citizens Regardless of Religious Affiliation (Articles 1, 4, 5, and 28). Article 4 declares: "Citizens of the USSR are equal under the law in all fields of civic, political, economic, social, and cultural life regardless of their attitude toward religion." Unless a citizen desires it, official documents are not to indicate the citizen's attitude toward religion.

Though religious organizations are not permitted to "participate in the activity of political parties" or give them financial assistance, "ministers of religious organizations have the right to participate in political life on an equal footing with all citizens" (Article 5).

Right to Foreign Religious Contacts (Articles 9 and 24). Article 24 guarantees citizens and religious organizations "the right to establish and maintain, on either a group or individual basis, international ties and direct personal contact." Soviet citizens may pursue religious studies abroad.

Registration of Religious Groups (Articles 7-16). One of the most ambiguous sections of the new law has to do with registration. Which organizations must register and according to what criteria will the state decide whether to register them or not? What is clear is that for an organization to have juridical status it must be registered. What this means in practice is uncertain. It may mean that under present circumstances unregistered groups will be left alone, but that in a property dispute, for example, they would not have recourse to the law and courts. But the fuzziness of all this leaves open the possibility of considerable arbitrary government behavior in the future.

International Treaties Take Precedence over Soviet Law (Article 31). "If an international treaty to which the USSR is a signatory has established rules other than those contained in the legislation on freedom of conscience and religious organizations, the rules of the international treaty shall apply." This is very encouraging, and yet it is disappointing that more of the specific and unambiguous international law language was not utilized in the text of the October 1990 law.

A *"state organ for religious affairs"* (Article 29). Apparently the Council for Religious Affairs is going to be replaced by a new agency which has yet to be named. The organization is to be an "informational, consultative, and expert center" which will maintain contacts with similar agencies on the republic level, serve as a data bank on religious organizations and the implementation of the Law on Freedom of Conscience, establish an "expert council" for responding to requests for information from the state or courts, serve as liaison between the state and religious groups, and promote religious tolerance and interreligious harmony.

Several observations need to be made regarding the new law. First, the existence of legal protections and fair procedures does not guarantee their implementation. As imperfect as Soviet law has been, even where it did offer some protection of rights in the past, they were often absent in a political world dominated by administrative arbitrariness. This makes all the more troubling the insufficient and inconsistent provision for the right of appeal in the proposed law.

Second, the rights of religious believers are more clearly and more specifically set out in the international agreements the Soviet Union has signed. It is a shame that more of the explicit definition of the rights of believers from these covenants is not included in the proposed Soviet law.

Third, the whole notion of the legitimacy of registration needs to be challenged. There is real reason to fear that the past attempts to control the religious organizations has not come to an end. Particularly ominous is Article 16 which allows for the termination of a religious organization if it violates "the provisions of this law or other laws of the USSR." And who will decide if this "violation" occurs? The only solution for this problem is to recognize the religious organization's right to exist as something which does not require the permission of government.

We in the West, even the so-called experts, have been so impressed by obvious improvements with the new law that we have not always paid sufficient attention to some Russian voices who are a good deal more skeptical. Gleb Anishchenko, one of the leaders of the Christian Democrat movement, penned a penetrating challenge to the spirit behind the apparently progressive proposed Law on the Freedom of Conscience. Anishchenko's contention is that the architects of the new law were attempting to put a "human face" on communism. The attempt to destroy the church failed, so now the concerted effort is to control it, to use it even more effectively than in the past. When all is said and done, it is still government officials who require registration and decide who is registered and who is not.

Even if Anishchenko is right that some of the chief architects of the new law still want to promote communism and to manipulate the church in more subtle and sinister ways than in the past, he ought to take comfort that the plan may well backfire. To give as much freedom to religious organizations as the new law does unleashes forces which may well overwhelm sinister efforts to control ecclesiastical bodies.

Despite these reservations, the new law is an important step towards conforming with international norms on religious freedom. An important measure of the depth of *glasnost* will be whether these formally approved changes in the law will be fully implemented.

RELIGIOUS LITERATURE BECOMES AVAILABLE IN THE SOVIET UNION

Only about 450,000 of the estimated 4.1 million Bibles or New Testaments which reached Soviet believers from 1945 through 1986 were legally imported or printed in the USSR. The vast majority of Scriptures were smuggled in or printed without permission. Between the late 1920s and 1956 there was an absolute ban on the printing of all Bibles in the Soviet Union.

In July 1983, Gederts Melngailis, a Latvian Lutheran, was arrested for distributing unofficial religious literature. He was sentenced to an indefinite term in a psychiatric hospital. Melngailis was freed in June 1988, and in that same year the *official* importation of Bibles to the Soviet Union was greater than all that had been legally imported to or printed there during the previous seventy years of Soviet rule. Religious literature of all sorts is now flowing into the Soviet Union both officially and unofficially.

Our group of American Christians visiting the USSR in the spring of 1988 was able to get some sense of the situation relative to the availability of and demand for religious literature. Everywhere we went, whether among the registered or unregistered Protestants, Catholics, or Russian Orthodox, the situation was the same—religious materials were becoming more available, but the needs still far exceeded the supply.

Rev. Arnis Silis, pastor of a charismatic Baptist church in Riga (Latvia), baptized fourteen new converts in 1988 at his church. Unfortunately, he was able to give a Bible to only half of that group; the other half went home empty-handed.

Even in Leningrad, which boasts one of the two largest Baptist churches in the Soviet Union, the gift of a Bible by our delegation invariably was greeted with hugs and often tears. In churches off the tourist trail, the absence of Bibles is often a much more serious problem.

For example, a young Methodist pastor in Estonia told us that in the previous five years he had not had a single spare copy of the Bible to give to those who wanted to learn more about the Christian faith. He did say his church had a "loaner" Bible and most of his church families had a Bible.

On two separate occasions we were told—once by a believer, once by a Soviet official—that at least some Bibles legally imported to registered Russian Orthodox and Baptist churches had been sold for between thirty-five and one hundred roubles (approximately 55 to 160

U.S. dollars at the official exchange rate at that time) by the denominations involved. It was not clear if this was to meet church funding problems, or a consequence of clergy corruption, but it certainly was another manifestation that demand for Bibles outstrips supply.

Soviet officials often cited the recent granting of permission to import Bibles and commentaries as evidence of past problems being solved. At Moscow Sheremetevo airport, however, our delegation encountered another side of the story. Customs officials confiscated four copies of three different pieces of religious literature, including the Bible. The person from whom the materials were taken explained that the materials were gifts for members of churches he planned to visit during the millennium year celebration. But customs officials simply confiscated them as illegal contraband.

When we later reported the incident to Soviet officials at *Znanie* (Knowledge)—an organization which specialized in propagating atheism for over four decades—we were told that decisions made at the center favoring greater openness were sometimes slow to reach customs officials. It is hard to believe, however, that if religious literature is no longer considered a threat to state security, a simple directive to customs officials would not settle the matter. Clearly, such an unequivocal directive had not been sent or was not being enforced.

Though permits still seem to be required for most large-scale deliveries of Bibles and religious literature, there is much less concern about whether they will be obtained than there was in the past. In October 1990 it was reported that the World Home Bible League had received permission from Ukrainian government officials to import "unlimited quantities" of Christian literature. Furthermore, a first shipment of 340,000 Bibles, New Testaments, and Gospel portions were to be delivered to *unregistered* Baptists and Pentecostals. Usually the requirement has been that there be a recognized (registered) church body to receive the Scriptures. In September 1989, a Soviet official even requested that Slavic Gospel Press import fifty million Bibles into the Soviet Union. At present there appears to be more openness by Soviet authorities for religious materials to be imported than there is commitment by Western Christians to do so.

In November 1989, one of the most unusual requests for Bibles was tendered. The head of the Soviet Children's Fund, Albert Likhanov, approached the International Bible Society (Colorado Springs, Colorado) and asked for four million Scriptures. The

Children's Fund is a broad, humanitarian organization set up in the USSR in 1987 to help orphans and families. The Children's Fund wanted to give the Bibles to any of their donors who request them. The IBS agreed to print one million of the New Testaments, and to do so on a Soviet printing press.

In 1990 the Evangelical Christian Publishers Association, in cooperation with the Christian Booksellers Association, television and radio ministries, and other groups, launched "The Moscow Project," a $1.6 million program to provide four million Russian-language scriptures by the time the next International Moscow Book Fair is held in September 1991.

A host of other mission organizations and parachurch groups have set goals for Bible distribution. In early March 1990, five trucks from Sweden rolled into Zaoksky with printing equipment, and later that month the formal founding of the Adventist Publishing House occurred. This is the first printing house in the Soviet Union owned and managed by a religious organization. Plans were to have the printing facility operational by the end of 1990, and to concentrate initially on the production of Bibles.

One of the most requested religious items in the Soviet Union is a children's Bible, nor is its use exclusively for children. In fact, many adults who have little if any background in the Bible prefer to read a children's Bible because the simpler form makes it easier to follow the general outline of events and the spiritual truths which are communicated. A number of mission organizations have been providing children's Bibles, and now the United Bible Societies is involved with this as well.

Beginning in November 1988, the Soviet monthly journal *V Mire Knig* (The World of Books) began publishing sections of the New Testament. The foreword to the first installment contained the following words of Professor Sergei Averintsev: "One cannot but rejoice that the triumph of common sense in our society has made this publication possible." With a print run of over 100,000, and assuming that each issue is read by several people, the potential impact of such a publication is great.

As important as it is to provide Soviet believers with the Bible, another serious problem relates to the dearth of other religious literature: study materials, commentaries, concordances, Bible dictionaries, apologetic material. Here, too, there have been major breakthroughs. One of the most impressive and sensitive projects carried out by Western Christians involved choosing and translating a multi-volume commentary for the Soviet Protestant community. To determine which commentary would be most compatible with the needs of Russian Christians, translations were obtained of eight different Protestant commentaries of the Epistle to the Romans. The All-Union Council of Evangelical Christians-Baptists (AUCECB) studied the alternatives and decided that William Barclay's version was the most readable and practical, though at certain points there were interpretations which the Russian community deemed insufficiently conservative. It was decided simply to leave out the offending passages.

In 1987 and 1988, five thousand copies of the fifteen-volume commentary were delivered to the All-Union Council of Evangelical Christians-Baptists, and an additional five thousand copies were sent during the middle of 1989. A translation is now underway of the Barclay Old Testament commentaries.

And this is not all. Religious literature is no longer getting into the country only through large, officially-approved Western shipments. The first crack in the literature barrier came in September 1987 when Moscow customs officials announced that new postal regulations would allow up to three religious publications to be mailed to Soviet citizens. As of September 1, 1988, customs tariffs were reduced on packages arriving from abroad, and many items may now be sent into the USSR without charge. The list of items which private citizens may receive from abroad has greatly expanded. A high-ranking customs official stated: "One may even send religious literature, which formerly was quite categorically forbidden." Small packages of religious literature are getting through with high regularity.

Slavic Gospel Association (SGA) provides an excellent example of a mission group taking advantage of the opportunities afforded by *glasnost* to send religious literature into the Soviet Union. In addition to truck loads of books, during much of 1988 SGA sent 440-pound pallets of Bibles and Christian books three times a week into the USSR. Such a shipment would typically include a hundred Bibles and five hundred Christian books.

In fiscal year 1989, SGA mailed or shipped in one million Bibles or portions. But in the next nine months it sent in 3.1 million pieces of literature, almost 90 percent of which were Scriptures. During the next two months, another half million pieces of literature went in.

Even before this large surge in literature shipments, SGA was receiving between two thousand and three thousand letters a month in its Frankfurt and Wheaton offices. Other ministries are also reporting a dramatic rise in correspondence with both believers and nonbelievers in the USSR. The overwhelming request is for Bibles and Christian literature. Requests for religious literature also are being generated by radio broadcasting into the Soviet Union. Unfortunately, in recent months SGA reports a decline in the number of letters received, which may well indicate governmental interference.

Elsewhere in the church world discussions are now in process which may result in joint-venture publishing between the Soviets and Westerners. Evangelical publishers were at the 1985, 1987, and 1989 Moscow International Book Fairs. At the 1989 Fair, the Evangelical Christian Publishers Association (ECPA) tested the limits of *glasnost* by distributing ten thousand copies of the New Testament. Though fair officials were not pleased, and scolded ECPA leaders in private, they did not interfere with the distribution of the Testaments. Each morning huge lines formed of Soviets anxious to obtain a New Testament. A few booths down, Madalyn O'Hair fumed in her American Atheist Press booth about the danger American evangelicals posed for *glasnost*.

But it was clear that the Soviets jammed into the bookfair did not agree with O'Hair's sentiments. They were weary of atheism, and when the ten thousand Testaments were gone, seventeen thousand more Soviets left their names and addresses in hopes that one would be mailed to them. The World Bible Translation Center, whose translation had been distributed, complied with those requests in the weeks following the event.

Though officially the ban on bringing in religious literature has been lifted, word of this has not always reached the borders. While officials are agreeing to the legal import of millions of copies of Bibles and publishing Solzhenitsyn in large quantities in their journals, at customs one can enter a time warp and step back into another era. In 1989 and 1990 there continued to be reports of harassment and confiscations of literature.

Although Soviet customs officials do continue to be arbitrary and somewhat erratic, huge amounts of religious literature are being allowed through. Much of the literature contains an address of the sender and tens of thousands of letters are being received by numerous mission organizations thanking them for the packages.

In general, the proliferation of opportunities to provide religious literature in the Soviet Union is breathtaking. The remaining obstacles and problems are real, but not nearly as real as the numerous doors now open that Bible societies and the suppliers of religious literature are just beginning to explore. In light of this, the severely depleted Western stockpiles of religious literature in Russian and other languages spoken in the Soviet Union is a major cause for concern.

THE RECOVERY OF EXILED RUSSIAN RELIGIOUS THOUGHT

In one of the most significant religious decisions of the Gorbachev era, the Politburo of the Communist Party Central Committee voted on May 12, 1988, to allow publication over the next three to four years of some of the classic works of late nineteenth and twentieth century Russian religious thinkers. Now these Christian thinkers can acquire the much broader readership they deserve, and more importantly, a culture very much adrift can begin to come to terms with some impressive theological ballast from a not so distant, but forbidden past.

The recovery of Russia's own religious literature and culture is an important part of any future religious renaissance in that part of the Soviet Union. Each of the peoples of the Soviet Union must reclaim the spiritual heritage which is uniquely its own.

These strides toward religious freedom, as remarkable as they are, do not tell the whole story. In the next chapter we will see other developments which are at least as surprising.

CHAPTER 7

THE IMPACT
OF *GLASNOST*
ON CHRISTIAN BELIEVERS
PART II

THE HEALING TOUCH OF THE CHURCH

*F*or almost a quarter of a century before Mikhail Gorbachev came to power, the Council for Religious Affairs was headed by a man who wrote that "church charities have no practical value at all." Vladimir Kuroedov also asserted that "charity by the church is clearly absurd; charitable work by religious organizations in our country cannot be carried on because it has nothing whatsoever to do with satisfaction of the religious needs of people."

One of the first appeals to appear in the Soviet press for a change in the official stance occurred in March 1987, more than a year before Baptist parishioners were allowed to begin volunteer efforts. The popular author Daniel Granin explained the demise of charity: "Charity has not declined by accident; it was systematically obliterated during the time of the dispossession of the *kulaks*, when people were not allowed to help the victims, and sentiments like charity were regarded as suspect." (The kulaks were well-to-do peasants deliberately stripped of their wealth in the early 1930s in a state campaign to collectivize agriculture.) Granin challenged Soviet citizens to become involved in charity once again.

Granin did not just talk about the importance of *miloserdie* (mercy, charity) he did something about it. Beginning in Leningrad in April 1988, his *Miloserdie* Society spread throughout the Soviet Union, and by December an All-Union *Miloserdie* Society was founded. Typical of the kind of activity sponsored by *Miloserdie* was the "Day of Mercy" in the Kaluga region southwest of Moscow. Clothing, bed-linen, and over a thousand pairs of shoes were donated by local factories and given to the elderly and others in need. Though by no means exclusively Christian, there has been prominent Christian participation in *Miloserdie.*

Baltic believers have led the way in the Christian charity movement. In December 1988, the Latvian Christian Mission was organized under the leadership of Vladimir Kovalev. This innovative group has combined humanitarian assistance with Christian evangelism. By early 1990, the 250 members of this group were working in seven hospitals, three children's homes, and several homes for the elderly. It was also providing a "meals-on-wheels" service for 200 elderly or disabled, as well as running a soup kitchen in Riga for those in need. They have plans to build a hospital, a children's home, a facility for the elderly, and a prisoner rehabilitation center.

In early 1988 members of the Moscow Baptist church approached Valentin Kozyrev, chief physician of the Kashchenko mental hospital, with an unusual proposal. Would he allow volunteers from the church to work in the hospital? Kozyrev immediately agreed, and in April 1988 fifty Baptist women began to visit the hospital daily to take care of patients, clean, and do other odd jobs.

Beginning in June 1988, members of the Yelokhovsky Cathedral, the patriarchal cathedral, became volunteers in the neurology department of Basmanov Hospital. One of the hospital officials exclaimed, "they're an absolute godsend." Indeed, that is precisely how the Christian volunteers wanted to be viewed. Within a year two other Moscow Orthodox congregations joined in the work, and churches in other cities are becoming involved as well.

In part, hospital authorities are simply responding to the desperate need for support personnel. Kharchev put the shortfall at twenty thousand in a speech to party workers in 1988. But some Soviet officials seem genuinely to recognize the unique value of religious volunteers. Dr. Kozyrev spoke of the necessity of "chemistry plus love" in the treatment of mental patients: "And if we as doctors and scientists are able to fulfill the first part of this formula to some extent, we are virtually incapable of fulfilling the second part, which is love."

That such cooperation between a state hospital and a church is possible is a marked departure from the past. All charitable institutions were nationalized in 1918, and from 1929 there was a formal prohibition against all organized religious charitable activity. Though the prohibition was still on the books, its practical abolition began in 1988, and it was formally abolished in 1990.

Nowhere is the need any greater or the contribution of the church more significant than that of ministry to children. And of course, nowhere did the old Communist regime fight more fiercely to limit the involvement of the church. In fact, the Communist authorities even engaged as late as the 1970s in the hideous crime of taking some children away from the Christian parents, in order to "save" them from the "pernicious" impact of a religious upbringing.

During the *glasnost* period the Soviets themselves have begun to discuss the tragic plight of many children in their society. In late 1989, for example, a Soviet publication revealed that 1.1 million children were in orphanages (*internats*).

Metropolitan Mefodi of Voronezh has played a key role in mobilizing Orthodox involvement in children's work. The Patriarchate's workshops at Sofrino, which produce ecclesiastical goods for the church, have become a patron of a Moscow children's home and are providing clothes, televisions, bicycles, and other items for the children. The metropolitan has played a key role in urging adoption of these neglected children. Particularly difficult is the task of dealing with profoundly disturbed children, but Moscow clergy have taken up this task. Where once there was great despair, now there are glimpses of Christian hope.

Sadly, the response in the Orthodox church to the new opportunities for humanitarian ministry has not been all that it might have been. This is the 1989 assessment of the Journal of the Moscow Patriarchate, not previously inclined to self-criticism:

> Many parishioners who had taken up charitable work on the spur of the moment abandoned it within a month or two. Some of them, especially young people, proved to be unprepared psychologically for the sight of the suffering of the gravely sick and dying. The dispersion of believers in the parishes and lack of contact with the local clergy also have a negative effect. The inertia of the stagnation period is still there. The church's estrangement from public life, the blame for which was not hers, resulted in believers adopting a guarded attitude towards society. Today, when the conditions for public activity by Christians are favorable, many of us are not ready for it morally.

Despite these legitimate concerns, even the sometimes modest Orthodox and Protestant response to new opportunities for service to society is providing much needed relief for thousands of individuals, and hope for many thousands more.

It would be a mistake to conclude that church charitable activities did not exist in the pre-Gorbachev Soviet era. They did—though they had to be done very quietly and there was always the threat of interference by the authorities. The Council for Religious Affairs frequently complained in the 1960s and 1970s that the churches were engaged in charitable activities.

Charity is nothing new for Russian Christians. What is new are the opportunities to engage in it openly and the larger scale which is allowed.

WESTERN INVOLVEMENT IN SOVIET CHARITY

In February 1990, Hannu Haukka (International Russian Radio/TV), in cooperation with Pat Robertson's Christian Broadcasting Network, had just brought fifty thousand syringes and other medical supplies into the Soviet Union to be distributed through the Baptist union. The chief doctor of the Russian Republic Children's Hospital stunned Haukka by going well beyond simply thanking the Western group for the medical supplies when he asked, "But do you have anything to also meet the spiritual needs of the children?" Within minutes the Finnish ministry had agreed to supply thirteen hundred children's Bibles—one for each bed in the hospital.

The 1986 Chernobyl nuclear disaster occurred prior to many of the major *glasnost* breakthroughs, and thus Western offers of help were often viewed with great suspicion, even by Soviet church figures. Metropolitan Filaret of Minsk declared in May 1986 that foreigners were simply trying to "gain political advantage from someone else's grief." But there was more openness to offers of help following the December 1988 Armenian earthquake. By April 1990, approximately $6 million worth of humanitarian assistance had been given by Western Christian organizations to aid in the recovery. In the wake of the momentous 1989/90 changes in Eastern Europe, the Salvation Army is reestablishing its work in the Baltics, having returned to Riga in May 1990. In 1991, World Vision is opening an office in Moscow.

One of the most positive examples of outside Christian involvement in the Soviet Union during the *glasnost* era has been the arrival of Mother Teresa's Missionaries of Charity. In the fall of 1987, Mother Teresa was refused permission to establish her ministry in the Soviet Union. But she stubbornly kept pressing her request, and was allowed to make her first visit to the Soviet Union in December 1988, following the Armenian earthquake. By the following June she had made two more visits to the USSR, centers had been opened in Armenia and Georgia, and thirteen sisters were working in Moscow.

As of July 1990, an estimated two thousand legally recognized Soviet independent philanthropic organizations had come into existence. By no means are all, or even most of these groups, exclusively religious.

FLOWERING OF INDIGENOUS EVANGELISM

Much attention in the West has been paid to the increasingly normal sight of Western evangelists and Christian leaders traveling to the Soviet Union. We are much less aware of the activities of the Soviet peoples themselves to send out missionaries and to evangelize. It is an impressive and inspiring part of the story, and if we understood it better, and if more Western Christian groups were aware of the indigenous efforts which are underway, there could be even more coordination between Christians in the Soviet Union and abroad in carrying out the Great Commission.

Not since the 1920s has it been possible to hold outdoor evangelistic services and openly invite nonbelievers to attend. In Kiev, however, in 1988 local authorities permitted a Baptist church to host an evangelistic service attended by four thousand people. More than one hundred made a public commitment to Christ. Later that same day, other Baptist churches in Kiev held an outdoor revival service along the Dnieper River. Five thousand gathered to listen. When the local militia tried to interfere, the crowd insisted the service be allowed to continue, and the militia backed off. On the next day, Sunday, Kievan believers conducted a baptismal service attended by more than ten thousand. Seventy-five were baptized.

Slavic Gospel Association has received many reports from throughout the Soviet Union regarding open-air baptismal services and evangelistic meetings. One Soviet believer wrote to tell of a meeting on May 1-2, 1988, attended by 1,500 young people. He reported that 120 were converted. A Christian in Estonia reported meetings in local parks, though there was often a shortage of

Christian literature to give out.

In January 1989 the Moscow Baptist church rented a hall for two evangelistic meetings. Two thousand attended and 120 made commitments to Christ. The AUCECB general secretary reported in March that within the last few months there were sixteen meetings like it.

Throughout the Soviet Union groups within congregations, particularly Protestant ones, are organizing themselves into local outreach or missionary societies. One of the earliest important mission societies to be formed is Gospel Light, founded in February 1989 in the city of Rovno (two hundred miles northwest of Kiev). Most of its work is in Ukraine, but some is in Estonia, and the work in Siberia is becoming ever more important. There is also interest in taking the mission to Muslims in Central Asia.

Some of the Gospel Light staff travel from city to city showing the film *Jesus*. In August 1989, missionaries went into one Ukrainian city, rented a cultural center, and sold tickets to eleven hundred nonbelievers for a concert by a sixty-eight-voice choir. On stage hung the communist slogan: "The Party is the mind, the honor, and the conscience of our time." The missionaries draped over it: "Jesus is the hope of the world." After the concert, the local Council for Religious Affairs head remarked: "This is exactly the message our nation needs to hear!"

In June 1989, the Evangelism Center was founded in a suburb of Moscow. Later that year I attended their weekly Old Testament Bible study. Peter Sautov, head of the Center, gave a fine presentation to a group of twenty to twenty-five, fielding queries from nonbelievers with great sensitivity. Two of those present, one of whom was a student at Moscow State University, had just become Christians as a result of the Luis Palau meetings in Moscow a few days before. They were given the mission society's last two copies of the "Four Spiritual Laws." The leaders of the Evangelism Center explained to me that because of a shortage of religious literature, it was necessary for nonbelievers who wished to pursue religious questions further to come to the center to read the Bible and related materials. Sautov also reported that he had been preaching on the Arbat (a central area of Moscow) for three years, but just two weeks before he had been taken in by the authorities and warned that if he did not stop, he could be sent to prison. He did not seem worried; these things run in cycles, he commented, and for some reason September was often a rough month.

Another form of evangelism is Christian apologetics as practiced in debates with atheists. In the past, genuine public dialogue between atheists and believers has been rare. A number of stimulating and fair debates, however, have occurred during the Gorbachev era.

In Donetsk, in south Russia, believers were allowed to stage a series of debates between pastors and professors of atheism. Topics included the existence of God and the influence of religion on Russian culture. Up to one thousand attended each debate, and the pastors gave an excellent account of their side of the argument. Even some factory bosses have allowed discussions to occur between Christians and atheist teachers.

Rev. Alexander Volokitkin, one of two principal pastors of the registered Leningrad Baptist church, has reported that since 1986 his church had been in dialogue with local atheists. Discussions were conducted in a civil and respectful manner. Members of the Leningrad atheist clubs have visited the church, and Rev. Volokitkin chaired a public meeting outside the church. The session was well attended by both Christians and nonbelievers. Atheists cordially asked many questions of the believers.

Dialogue sessions also occurred in 1988 in several cities in Soviet Central Asia. Local officials were particularly interested in why believers had more stable marriages and why their young people were able to avoid drugs and alcohol. The officials even noticed that the young believers paid social visits on the elderly. Serious moral *perestroika* of Soviet society requires that the positive social fruits of a believer's lifestyle be considered seriously.

Christians in the Soviet Union know the words of Jesus: "The harvest is plentiful but the workers are few. Ask the Lord of the harvest, therefore, to send out workers into his harvest field" (Matthew 9:37-38). They are working hard on their own, and as the next section will describe, they are cooperating with Western Christians in an effort to bring the gospel to millions of Soviet citizens weary of atheist indoctrination.

WESTERN INVOLVEMENT IN EVANGELISM

On a remarkable evening in the summer of 1988, ten thousand young people jumped to their feet at the Leningrad Sports Complex to cheer and clap their approval of a riveting American rock ballet. In a creative combination of mime, music, dance, and narration, a cast of thirty had just completed the last of eighteen performances in

Moscow and Leningrad. This was not the first American show to visit this place; Billy Joel had performed there in 1987. But the 1988 production was very different.

The Toymaker's Dream is not just another rock opera. Its message is explicitly Christian and traces in unmistakable detail the biblical account of the creation of Adam and Eve, the Fall, the coming of Christ, His crucifixion, and His resurrection. The narration was in Russian.

Advertised with pictures in the local press, the production eventually played to a total of seventy-five thousand Soviet citizens. Some of the proceeds went to support a Soviet/American peace program. But the troupe was in the Soviet Union to perform, not make one-sided political statements about arms control. Enthusiastically received throughout their engagement, the Tulsa-based Impact Productions show was invited to return to the USSR in 1989.

Though *The Toymaker's Dream* has been performed all over the world for several years, the show's producer, Tom Newman, considers their 1989 tour to the Soviet Union the most significant of their history. The production was performed a total of twelve times in Tallinn, Kiev, and Moscow. More openly evangelistic than the first time, and engaged in considerable Scripture distribution, the trip was not without its tense moments. After their first performance in Kiev, the mayor and the director of concerts for the city angrily confronted Newman with the assertion that in the USSR Jesus could be proclaimed only in churches, not in public arenas. They threatened to turn off the power the next night if open evangelization again took place.

But the production was repeated without change the next night to a wildly enthusiastic audience of seventeen thousand, and the power remained on. The director of programs even apologized for his earlier comments. By the time the cast returned to the United States the show had been covered on national television four times, and had been written about in *Pravda*, as well as in the Ukrainian and Estonia press.

The Soviet Union is a land of anomalies. While customs agents at the Moscow airport still occasionally confiscate religious literature, night after night a Christian rock ballet downtown can blaze out the gospel message. There is more openness under Mr. Gorbachev than under his predecessors, but the openness has sometimes been like walking on an iced-over pond in springtime. Just when you think your footing is solid, you plunge into the chilly waters beneath the surface. New opportunities are sprinkled in unpredictably amidst the old restrictions and prohibitions.

Take for example radio broadcaster Earl Poysti's June 1990 evangelistic tour through Eastern Siberia, including cities which had been closed to foreigners. No foreign evangelists had previously spoken in Vladivostok, but Poysti addressed a packed auditorium in the "Lenin House of Culture." Atheist professors from the local university were present, and Bibles for their library were accepted with appreciation. In Ussurisk, Poysti preached in the city of his birth, where his father Nikolai in the 1920s had conducted evangelistic services. The city of Tynda had no churches and no known believers, but the mayor of the city arranged for them to visit, a service was broadcast over local television, and the mayor gave permission for a church to be built in the city. In Chita, Poysti's first service was in a prison. Throughout the trip Poysti met Soviet citizens who had listened to his broadcasts from abroad for many years. For a man who had left the Soviet Union as a boy in 1927 and had been involved in radio ministry to the Soviet Union since 1946, such a return to his native land was a dream come true.

In 1971 astronaut Jim Irwin was walking on the moon. Seventeen years later he was preaching in the Soviet Union. For many, the former is easier to imagine than the latter. Invited by the autonomously registered Baptists of Kiev, Riga, and Brest, Irwin in November 1988 preached the gospel in nine churches in ten days.

More than a thousand people came forward seeking salvation during Irwin's brief visit, and more than thirty thousand filled out requests for religious literature. Irwin also distributed ten thousand copies of his own testimony in Russian, prepared by Slavic Gospel Association. Irwin's trip was covered by Soviet TV and print media, and he met Soviet cosmonauts and scientists.

Significantly more opportunities are available to Christians in the Soviet Union to travel abroad than ever before. About seventy representatives from the USSR participated in the Second International Congress on World Evangelization in Manila held in mid-July 1989. Most were Baptists, but there were also some Pentecostals and Russian Orthodox. The Soviet delegation was unusual in that it was not just Protestants associated with the large predominantly Baptist union who were allowed to attend. There were autonomously registered Protestants, as well as some unregistered.

Unfortunately, some unregistered Pentecostal leaders such as Anatoly Vlasov and Ivan Fedotov, who were invited by the Lausanne Committee on World Evangelization organizers, were refused permission to attend by Soviet officials. Several weeks after the Lausanne meetings, Fedotov showed me with great disappointment his official invitation and the speech he had planned to give had he been permitted to attend the international gathering.

Soon after the Manila conference, Soviet and Western church leaders began making plans for a major evangelism conference in Moscow. The Lausanne Committee, Leighton Ford Ministries, and Issachar Frontier Missions Strategies organized the Soviet Congress on Evangelization (October 22-26, 1990). The remarkable gathering attracted 152 non-Soviets from twenty-four countries, and approximately 1100 Soviet participants from all fifteen Soviet republics. Representatives were present from Orthodox, Catholic, and a wide variety of Protestant groups. Members of both registered and unregistered churches were in attendance.

In September 1989, Argentine-born American evangelist Dr. Luis Palau preached to forty thousand people in Moscow, Leningrad, Kishinev, Riga, and Kiev. Graced by the excellent interpretive skills of fellow evangelist Viktor Hamm, Palau was well received and invitations were immediately extended to return to the Soviet Union for future evangelistic campaigns.

Baptist, Pentecostal, Lutheran, and Adventist churches in the Leningrad area combined forces for a three-day evangelism crusade October 19-21, 1990. Each night twenty-one thousand people packed into the city's Lenin Sports and Entertainment Complex to hear Finnish evangelist Kalevi Lehtinen. One hundred thousand New Testaments were imported for distribution during the campaign. Copies of "The Four Spiritual Laws" were also given out. In preparation for the crusade, one thousand Soviet Christians attended a ten-hour training course in counseling, and every home in the city received an invitation to come to the meetings.

Video evangelism is also beginning to hit the USSR. Requests for video equipment, blank videos (which cost up to $100 on the black market), and Christian videos are increasingly heard from contacts within the Soviet Union. The authorities have reacted with considerably more tolerance in the Baltic states, Leningrad, and Moscow to the use of religious videos than they have in the Central Asian republics. The videos "Jesus" and "Superbook" are being widely seen in the USSR. In addition, Slavic Gospel Association has prepared several of the Moody Science films in Russian. These and other tapes are already circulating within the Soviet Union.

PRISON EVANGELISM

The chronicles of Christians languishing in Soviet prisons are filled with the special punishment so often meted out to those who were caught with but a single page of the Gospel or who sought to share their faith with fellow prisoners. But beginning in 1989, Christian groups have been regularly invited into Soviet correctional institutions to conduct religious services.

One of the principal objectives of the Latvian Christian Mission, founded in late 1988, is evangelizing and rehabilitating prisoners. The Protestant mission regularly visits six penal colonies in Latvia. Their musical group, *Rozhdestvo* (Christmas) has toured Siberia and included in their itinerary a number of labor camps. In early 1990, the mission held an evangelism conference which brought together representatives of sixty-four churches and five new missionary societies. The conference was also attended by the governors of three Latvian penal colonies, who reported on the positive impact of the Christian ministry on the prisoners.

At about the same time that Protestants were becoming involved in prison ministries, the Orthodox were as well. In July 1989, at the invitation of Ukrainian government officials, Metropolitan Filaret of Kiev was invited to visit a maximum-security prison (Bucha) near Kiev. The author of an article in *Literaturnaia Gazeta* (Literary Gazette) reporting on the visit noted that this was the first time in seventy years that a priest had visited a labor camp without being an inmate. Filaret addressed over seven hundred prisoners and there was a warm response to his presence. Camp officials said that henceforth any religious literature would be allowed into the camp, prisoners could wear crosses, and a room would be set aside where a priest could hear confession and administer the sacraments.

In April 1990, Charles Colson, head of Prison Fellowship, visited the Soviet Union as part of an official U.S. delegation. They visited five prison facilities, including some never before seen by foreigners. In a meeting with then Minister of Internal Affairs Bakatin, Colson learned that there was a 38 percent rise in crime in the Soviet Union in 1989. When Bakatin heard Colson describe the activities of Prison Fellowship, he enthusiastically responded: "That's what we need in

Russia." He continued: "What you are doing we will approve in the Soviet Union. . . . Whatever you need to do to get into our prisons, you have my permission. You are on to something that is important." Colson immediately set in motion plans to set up a Soviet branch of Prison Fellowship to help train Christians to minister to those in correctional facilities.

WESTERN CHRISTIAN INTERACTIONS WITH SOVIET SOCIETY

Christians from the West are not just involved in direct evangelism, religious literature distribution, or visiting fellow Christians. They are participating in educational exchanges, and a growing variety of direct person-to-person and organization-to-organization contacts. Christian lawyers, political scientists, historians, sociologists, philosophers, medical personnel, businessmen, and others are meeting with their often secular counterparts in the Soviet Union.

One of the most innovative projects which has emerged in the *glasnost* period involves setting up departments of Christian studies at secular universities. The International Institute for Christian Studies (Overland Park, Kansas) is negotiating doing this in a number of universities throughout Eastern Europe and the USSR. IICS provides the professors and their travel to the host country, and the university takes care of housing, office space, and other expenses associated with being part of the host institution. On July 26, 1990, the rector of Novosibirsk State University (central Siberia) gave his formal approval to IICS to set up a department at his university.

In October 1990, at a dinner in Washington, D.C. sponsored by the Christian College Coalition, I addressed a group of sixteen Soviet academics on the conflict between Russian culture and Soviet communism. After the dinner, several university administrators invited me to come to the USSR to lecture in their institutions, for several weeks if possible, on Christian apologetics, Russian culture, and democratic theory. The openness in the Soviet Union today to listen attentively to points of view which were previously forbidden is breathtaking.

On October 3, 1990, several colleges from the Christian College Coalition signed a protocol of intentions committing the American and Soviet institutions to seeking to work out student and faculty exchanges in the near future. The secular Soviet universities were very open to having Christian students on their campuses. Later that same month, Vladimir Kinelev, first vice-chairman of the State Committee on Science and Higher Education for the Russian Republic, proposed to John Bernbaum, vice-president of the Christian College Coalition, that the CCC establish a Christian college in Moscow.

One of the greatest opportunities for Christian influence in Soviet society is to expand Western Christian contacts with all dimensions of Soviet society, secular as well as Christian. Atheists and agnostics in the Soviet Union are far more open to religious ideas today than many of their secular counterparts in the West.

REOPENINGS AND REGISTRATIONS OF CHURCHES

It was a glorious day for Lithuanian Catholics. Vilnius Cathedral was reconsecrated on February 5, 1989, with thirty thousand witnesses packed into the cathedral square and before a Lithuanian television audience. Seized by the authorities in 1949 and used as an art gallery since the 1960s, Vilnius Cathedral is now once again serving as a place of worship.

Presiding at the reconsecration was Bishop Julijonas Steponavicius, himself a victim of many years of internal exile. Michael Bourdeaux, the one major foreign guest to witness this historic moment, described the significance of the occasion as follows:

> If there is one dominant impression . . . it was the quiet dignity of the whole massive crowd. Bishop Steponavicius personified this dignity; never in private or public a word of self-pity. Only an indication . . . that a regime of more than a quarter of a century of reading and prayer during his time of enforced exile, with only minimal contact with the world outside, had strengthened his faith.

Throughout the Gorbachev years, particularly beginning in 1987, Soviet and foreign coverage of *glasnost* has reported the return of many important cultural treasures to the Orthodox church. In November 1987 the Optina Pustyn monastery was returned. Built at the end of the eighteenth century, this famous home of the legendary startsy (elders) was a well-known pilgrimage site for writers such as Gogol, Tolstoy, and Dostoevsky.

The Monastery of the Caves in Kiev, founded in 1051, is considered one of the fountainheads of Slavic Christianity. Taken over by the secular authorities in 1961 and turned into a tourist attraction, parts of it were returned to the church during millennium festivities. In May 1990, extensive remaining portions of the historic monastery were returned to the church. The additional facilities will be used to expand the Kiev Theological Seminary, which was opened in the monastery in 1989.

One of the most spectacular signs of change was the June 1990 return to the Orthodox church of the largest cathedral in Leningrad— St. Isaac's. Completed in the mid-nineteenth century and with a capacity of thirteen thousand people, this remarkable church has been a museum for several decades. The reconsecration service was conducted by newly elected Patriarch Aleksy II and was attended by the president of the Russian republic, Boris Yeltsin. Parts of the service were shown on television and crowds on surrounding streets were so large that traffic was at a standstill for several hours. Unlike many other churches returned to the church, this was in good repair.

As exciting as the changes are in the Russian republic, transformations are sometimes more radical and sweeping in other republics, particularly the Baltics. On February 14, 1990, the Supreme Soviet of Lithuania approved (effective immediately) returning to its rightful owner all church property confiscated by the communists when they came to power forty-two years before. Present occupants of the buildings were given until July 1 to inform religious representatives of their schedule for vacating the premises. Beyond the return of old churches, occasionally new Orthodox facilities are being built.

Glasnost has encouraged some to pursue the recovery of their church buildings more energetically. On March 19, 1989, 300 people gathered in the town square of Ivanovo (150 miles northeast of Moscow) to demand the return of their church. The church was confiscated by the authorities in 1935 and turned into a repository for state archives. Two days later, four women began a hunger strike, and on March 30 the secretary of the town soviet told the strikers, "If there were a God, then we would open the church, but under the circumstances no one is prepared to open it for you."

A number of students who sought to help the women in the town square were beaten and fined ninety roubles each. On April 1 the women were forcibly hospitalized and fed intravenously. The women's protest attracted the attention of human rights activists elsewhere in the Soviet Union, and they pledged to join the hunger strike. On April 11 the women ended their strike after receiving a promise from the local government head that the fate of their church would be decided within a month. Finally, in mid-August, *Izvestiia* reported that the church had been turned over to the believers.

According to CRA official M. Mikhailov in 1990, there have been claims filed by groups of believers for the return of a total of eighteen thousand places of worship. Approximately five thousand of these buildings are in serious disrepair, while the rest are being used as museums, stores, shops, sports halls and so on.

Indeed, during 1989 the Public Commission for Giving Help to Christians (formed in May) began circulating an appeal to the Congress of Peoples' Deputies calling for "all" church buildings to be returned to the Russian Orthodox church. By August thousands of people had signed, including many prominent deputies, academics, church activists, writers, and artists.

Though there are many stubborn and difficult problems yet to be resolved as churches in the Soviet Union seek to regain full rights to their property, the ingenuity of some believers is impressive in providing for their needs. In the city of Kobrin, 600 miles southwest of Moscow not far from the Polish border, a Baptist congregation gained permission to tear down an abandoned Soviet army barracks. They had authorization to replace their old church with a new structure, but could not locate the necessary building supplies. For a nominal fee they were allowed to scavenge materials from the army barracks for their new building. As pastor Trubchik put it: "Thank God there is disarmament. Now churches are being built from materials which were previously used for war purposes."

EXPANDED EMIGRATION

Since the inception of the Soviet Union in 1917, approximately 15 million Soviet citizens or citizens of areas taken over by the USSR have been involved in out migrations from the USSR or Soviet-controlled territories. Though there have been many emigrations from the Soviet Union, scholarly literature has often focused on three well-known outflows. The first saw 1.5 million Russians flee the fledgling communist state between 1917 and 1922; the second exodus involved approximately 2 million displaced persons during World War II and its immediate aftermath; and the third (1948 through 1988) witnessed the departure of 553,100 in the three largest categories. The largest single group in this Third Emigration was the Jews

(318,500), followed by Germans (168,100), and Armenians (66,500). We may well be in the early stages of a "fourth" emigration.

According to TASS, in 1988, 108,000 Soviet citizens emigrated. *Pravda* has reported that the number who emigrated more than doubled in 1989 to 228,600. Jewish emigration hit its peak in the pre-*glasnost* period when, in 1979, 51,500 were allowed to leave. But then it steadily and rapidly declined, from 21,500 in 1980 to only 900 in 1986. But in 1987 the number jumped to 8,100, and in 1989 skyrocketed to 72,500. In the first ten months of 1990, over 120,000 left the Soviet Union. In late July 1990, Israel reported that it expected to receive a total of 150,000 Soviet Jews during the year.

As large as the recent numbers of Jewish emigres may seem, they may soon be dwarfed by much larger figures. Israelis at first talked of the possibility of one million Jews leaving the USSR by the end of 1995, but by September 1990, projections were being moved up to two million by the end of 1992, and the Israelis have reported that approximately one million visa applications requested by Soviet citizens within the past two to three years are still outstanding. Should such a mass exodus take place, no appreciable Jewish population would remain in the Soviet Union, even though it would be unlikely that so many could come out so quickly. Even at present rates of departure, by the year 2000 there would be almost no Jews left in the USSR.

One of the big surprises of 1988 was the sharp increase in Christian emigration, particularly among Pentecostals. In previous years, only a few dozen Baptists or Pentecostals managed to leave the Soviet Union, and then only after extended waits and much anguish. But according to World Relief, in fiscal years 1989 and 1990, almost 19,000 evangelicals arrived in the United States. This large influx of evangelical emigres from the Soviet Union is unprecedented for the Christian community.

For many years human rights activists in the West have pressed the Soviets to liberalize their emigration policy. Both Jews and Christians have sought emigration, but the former have been far more successful than the latter in achieving it.

Ever since the late seventies it had been clear that large numbers of Pentecostals (mainly unregistered) wanted to leave; estimates have often ranged from thirty thousand to seventy thousand. Two factors have motivated this desire to emigrate. First, the unregistered Pentecostals (there is a registered group as well), like all unregistered

Christians, have been subjected to considerable persecution. The issue of emigration became particularly pressing for many of them in the early 1960s during Khrushchev's antireligious campaign. In some cases, children were even taken away from Christian parents.

Second, many Pentecostals on the basis of Scripture and certain contemporary prophecies believe that a period of liberalization will be followed by a great persecution. They believe they must leave while they have the opportunity.

There is a serious misconception in the West that most unregistered Pentecostals want to leave. This is untrue. Most Pentecostals, like most other Christians in the USSR, would prefer to stay, and if *glasnost* continues to expand and does not follow the earlier, cyclical patterns of liberalization giving way to a new repression, the pressure to emigrate will undoubtedly lessen. Even if seventy thousand evangelicals did eventually leave the Soviet Union, that would be a relatively small number compared to the much larger group of Jews who have emigrated over the past decade.

The liberalized emigration policy of Gorbachev is a calculated risk. It rids the country of the most unhappy groups and individuals, while at the same time promoting the image abroad of a more humane Soviet Union. But the success of *glasnost* will be measured, in part, by whether the desire to emigrate significantly lessens. Most individuals opt to stay in their homeland unless driven out by repression or serious economic problems. And among Christians, many more will want to stay if they see even modest progress in achieving the religious freedom they desire for themselves and their children.

There are, however, some continuing problems for believers in the Soviet Union which will certainly effect their security and sense of well being in coming years. We now need to turn our attention to those aspects of Soviet reality which bear more resemblance to the past than to the more progressive aspects of the present.

EDUCATIONAL, ECONOMIC, AND POLITICAL DISCRIMINATION

Both before and during *glasnost* the official position has been that believers have not been and are not discriminated against. But as the Soviets are now admitting, Christians in many ways have been "second-class citizens," and even this they salvaged only by cooperating with the authorities in agreeing to restrict their religious activities and register with the government.

Though important officials and the press have made assuring statements that this discrimination is part of the past, it is not yet certain that it is. As late as 1989, Mark Elliott's assessment was still accurate:

> Perhaps the greatest single disability facing Christians in the USSR today is the ongoing, widespread, and systematic exclusion of them from higher education and preferred employment. Party membership, entailing an atheist oath, is a route to economic and social advancement not open to Christians.

Late in 1989, two Russian priests complained in *Moscow News* that, "It is an unwritten rule that a believer may not become a manager, a teacher or a military officer, and so on. Believers are second-class citizens." A former Communist Party member, present student at a Soviet military academy, and recent convert to Christianity wrote a letter to Ogonek (published in July 1990) protesting being barred from further educational studies. After six years of study, O. Nerodin (from Kharkov) lacked only two months before his exams to become an engineer. But though he was an excellent student, the authorities terminated his studies, according to the young man, "solely because I took a decision to believe in Jesus Christ."

The overall situation may be better than in the past, but there are still problems and believers remain concerned about whether the discrimination against them has really ended, despite the prohibitions against discrimination in the new Law on Freedom of Conscience.

ON IMPLEMENTING LEGAL GUARANTEES OF FREEDOM OF RELIGION

The official Soviet position is that it is a criminal offense to "refuse to give a citizen a job or to admit him to an educational establishment, to dismiss him from work or expel him from an educational establishment, to deprive him of benefits or advantages laid done by the law, or impose other significant restrictions on citizens' rights because of religious attitudes."

Surely there is some comfort to be taken from such a direct and uncompromising defense of believers' rights. But the statement does not date to the era of *glasnost* at all. It is a resolution from the Russian Soviet Federated Socialist Republic's Supreme Soviet Presidium, issued in March 1966—some nineteen years before Gorbachev took power.

The existence of this resolution and similar constitutional guarantees did not prevent the systematic and widespread violation of every guarantee listed. And during the Gorbachev era, significant evidence exists that in many parts of the USSR the rhetoric of legal guarantees has not been matched by the reality of religious freedom.

A believer from Novgorod wrote to the editors of *Izvestiia* in early March 1989 to complain that what believers in Leningrad and Moscow are allowed, believers in the provinces are not. In his case, he was dismissed from his duties as a teacher for reading his Bible during lunch break. He decided to abandon a career in education.

A high official in the Council for Religious Affairs responded with a frank admission that the CRA receives similar letters. He conceded that for years "obstacles have secretly been placed in the way of believers," resulting in them being treated as "second-class citizens." He assured the former teacher that such discrimination ought not to occur because legal guarantees are in place to protect him.

But religious *perestroika* is going to have to come to terms with this great discrepancy between paper guarantees and concrete realities.

SUSPICIOUS DEATHS

Amidst the swirl of good news coming out of the Soviet Union on expanded freedoms for believers, there have been some disturbing and sober reminders that the violence against Christians of earlier years is not entirely a thing of the past. According to Mark Elliott, fifteen Christian activists have been murdered or died in suspicious car accidents since 1986; ten of them alone died between April 1990 and February 1991. Nor is it always clear who the source of the violence is: KGB, extreme nationalists, common criminals, or genuine accidents.

As troubling as reported beatings, murders, and "accidents" are, it is important that we not jump to conclusions without studying each case individually and in the context of others which may be related to it. It is possible that some "accidents" really are accidents, though suspicions are justified in an atmosphere where threats of physical violence have occurred. Even if many of these deaths are not accidental, it does not follow that they were ordered by the central authorities. In most cases that is probably not what happened. It is far more likely that local KGB detachments or other local officials are behind the violence. Of course, to those Christians or human rights activists still targeted for such violence, it is little consolation that the order to strike at them originates locally, rather than with the central authorities.

In the economic, political, and social chaos into which the disintegrating USSR is sliding, there are other sources of violence besides the government. Extreme nationalist elements can react with dangerous force towards those with whom they differ. Anti-semites are not just a danger to Jews, but also to Christians and others who support or defend Jews. Violence against Ukrainian Catholics could also be vented against Orthodox or others who might defend the Ukrainian Catholics. Extremist Ukrainian Catholics could attack Russian Orthodox priests. In the volatile mix of factors which increasingly typifies the Soviet cauldron, it is not easy to say with certainty which deaths are "accidental," or in cases where foul play is established, who is responsible for it.

Unfortunately, one of the suspicious deaths involved an Orthodox friend with whom I had become acquainted just a month before his "accident."

Following the publication of *The Puzzle of the Soviet Church*, I traveled to Moscow in mid-September 1989 for the International Book Fair. While there I met an impressive human rights activist— Sergei Savchenko. On the third occasion Sergei and I were together, we attended a string quartet concert of baroque music along with my good friend Al Janssen, managing editor at Multnomah Press. Walking near the Kremlin after the concert was the last time we would ever see Sergei. One month and one day later, on October 23, Sergei was tragically killed when a car jumped onto the sidewalk and struck him.

What may have gotten Sergei into trouble was his participation in a fledgling Christian Democratic party, founded in early August by Alexander Ogorodnikov. It was at the apartment/office of this new group that I first met Savchenko.

Savchenko was a strong advocate of religious and political freedom. A relatively new convert to Christianity, he was a talented physicist and photojournalist. He intended to become involved in producing Christian television in the USSR. One of his most recent projects was a documentary book on the destruction of churches.

The circumstantial evidence pointing to foul play in Savchenko's death is strong. Between his "accident" and the time the morgue notified his friends, his entire photo archive of desecrated churches was stolen from his apartment. His death conveniently coincided with his wife being out of town. One of his best friends, the ambassador from Holland, was away as well.

Savchenko's "accident" was not the first time that someone close to Ogorodnikov had died under suspicious circumstances. Ogorodnikov's brother Raphael, a thirty-seven year old priest and monk, had died near Novgorod on November 18, 1988 in a car "accident." Even Anglican priest Dick Rodgers of London received veiled threats from Soviet officials because of his efforts to give Ogorodnikov a printing press.

In September 1989, when I met with Ogorodnikov and other editors of their samizdat journal, the *Bulletin of Christian Opinion*, I was told of the theft the previous April of a computer and subsequent beating in June of one of their journalists in Leningrad.

On November 7, the holiday celebrating the Bolshevik Revolution, Father Victor Grigoriev was left alone in the offices of the *Bulletin* to stand guard over their equipment. Through a ruse that could have succeeded only by tapping the phone, two strangers gained access to the apartment. They beat Grigoriev into unconsciousness, and stole three computers, two printers, and a fax machine.

At the time of Savchenko's death, suspicious accidents had already been reported in Lithuania, Rostov (on the Don), and in Georgia. In February 1986, Lithuanian Catholic priest Father Juozas Zdebskis, founder in 1978 of the Catholic Committee for Defense of Believers Rights died in a very suspicious car accident. According to the respected *Chronicle of the Lithuanian Catholic Church*, the collision was "a carefully planned and executed act of violence." Indeed, he had received a number of KGB threats, and had been the victim of other suspicious accidents in 1974 and 1980. In December 1988, Grigory Kushin, an editor of an underground Pentecostal journal, narrowly escaped death in a car "accident" in Ukraine. He had been threatened with violence if he did not cease his activities. Just ten days before Savchenko was killed in Moscow, one of the most prominent human rights activists died in a car "accident" in Georgia. Merab Kostava was a Georgian Orthodox, primarily involved in human rights and political protests, who had received death threats for several months, including one just before his death.

For many years Estonian Lutheran pastor Harald Meri had been conducting research into the Soviet deportation of Estonians to Siberia beginning with the 1940 annexation of this then independent Baltic state, and then again following the end of Nazi occupation. He also was investigating who had collaborated with the NKVD (the predecessor to the KGB) in the violence against his native land. Through the years he had received a number of death threats, but he continued his work anyway.

On April 5, 1990 Pastor Meri's home was destroyed by arson. At the same time both Meri and his housekeeper were reported missing. On Easter eve, April 14, their bodies were discovered about ten miles away in a forest. Autopsies revealed that both had been severely tortured, and the church consistently has charged that they were buried alive.

Nor has Latvia been spared. One of the vibrant signs of vitality in the Lutheran church in Latvia has been the emergence of the Rebirth and Renewal movement. This group of mainly young activists not only criticized those within the church hierarchy whom they felt were too compromised in their relations to church authorities, but they succeeded in obtaining new leadership. Thirty-four-year-old Pastor Armands Akmentins was involved with this group and was a theological student. On August 4, 1990, he was killed in an automobile accident near Riga. An autopsy revealed that he had multiple stab wounds in the back and had received blows to the head with a metal rod. In the car was found the identity card of a KGB officer who turned up two days later at a hospital with a concussion and abrasions, claiming he could remember nothing. A full explanation is not yet available as to what happened. Akmentins is survived by three small children and his wife. The car involved in the accident was a gift from the Latvian Evangelical Lutheran church in America.

Perhaps the most tragic unnatural death of the *glasnost* era is that of Father Alexander Men. In the early morning of September 9, 1990, this spiritual giant of Russian Orthodoxy was cut down by an axe in some woods between his home and the train station in Zagorsk. He was on his way to his church in Pushkino, about halfway between Zagorsk and Moscow.

Shock waves reverberated throughout Soviet society when news of the slaying became known. For though his name is not familiar to many Westerners, he was well known in the USSR as a powerful preacher, persuasive apologist for Christianity among the intellectuals, and friend of other Orthodox dissidents such as Gleb Yakunin. He was a close friend to the exiled author of *Gulag Archipelago*, Alexander Solzhenitsyn. But he was an author in his own right, having written ten books, including a six-volume study on the quest for truth and meaning in religion, and a children's book on the Bible, which became popular in Europe. Originally, at least, his works could not be published in the Soviet Union. He was also beloved by simple people who invariably warmed to his compassion, gentleness, and courage.

Accounts of his death appeared on television and in the press, and even Gorbachev before the parliament expressed "profound regret" at his passing demanding to know who would kill such a revered and innocent citizen. In the words of *Izvestiia*, "he was the pastor to many human-rights champions, prisoners of conscience, those who were persecuted by the authorities." But the newspaper went on to note that "his work in providing spiritual support to many intellectuals in disgrace brought him true friends, but also real foes."

And who were these enemies who could have plotted or rejoiced in the death of such a man? Father Gleb Yakunin is convinced that Men's death is "connected with the growing wave of anti-Semitism in Russia." Indeed, Men was Jewish by birth, and though for almost thirty years he had been an Orthodox priest, he strongly condemned both anti-Semitism and excessive Russian nationalism. But he had also strongly condemned the KGB through the years and other agencies of the government. In short, anti-Semites, Russian chauvinists, and the KGB all had reason to hate Father Alexander.

As so often has been the case in history, great men in life can sometimes become even more influential in death. Many who now daily visit Father Alexander's grave are fervently praying that this will be the case with this most recent martyr in a land rich with martyrs.

Continued violence against some Christian activists is deeply disturbing, and ought to be a warning to us not to assume that the problems of previous decades are no more. And yet, it would be a tragic mistake not to take seriously the massive evidence of dramatic improvements in dozens of areas affecting religious freedom and the life of the church. If the improvements continue, then the abusive and violent legacies of the past will stand out in ever more vivid contrast.

CONCLUSION

It has been said that the most dangerous moment for a bad government is when it begins to reform. Pent-up anger is unleashed, expectations rise faster than they can be fulfilled, and there is a general sense of unease.

On the other hand, there can be tremendous bursts of energy, excitement, and enthusiasm when genuine changes are allowed. With respect to religious believers, there is convincing evidence confirming the reality of *glasnost*.

Improvements are uneven and incomplete, but they are real. Opportunities exist for the church today, in the great majority of its denominational varieties, which were unheard of even five years ago.

Problems remain, some quite sinister. Yet, the general flow is in a positive direction. The aberrations, even the most violent ones, reflect standard operating procedures which dominated in earlier periods. The question now is which will win out—the rush towards liberalization or the stubborn holdout for an older, more repressive regime?

CHAPTER 8

ON PYRAMIDS, PARTHENONS, AND HOUSES OF CARDS
RELECTIONS ON THE FUTURE OF *GLASNOST* AND *PERESTROIKA*

> The Soviet system is made up of massive, heavy blocks. It is
> well suited to the suppression of human freedom, but not to
> revealing, nourishing and stimulating it. On the whole, it
> resembles an Egyptian pyramid built out of colossal stones,
> carefully assembled and ground to fit together. . . .
>
> Can you rebuild a pyramid into the Parthenon? The ancient
> Egyptian pyramids are rightly considered the most enduring
> of architectural forms—much more durable and solid than
> the Parthenon. And the legitimate question arises: Do
> pyramids lend themselves to *perestroika*?

*T*hese haunting words are those of Andrei Sinyavsky, one of the
most famous dissidents of the early Brezhnev era. After fifteen
years of living in the West, in early 1989 he was allowed to return to
the Soviet Union for five days following the death of his good friend
and fellow dissident Yuly Daniel.

Sinyavsky was struck by the changes he observed. There was
less fear and people talked far more openly than in the past. But the
shadow of the KGB was still everpresent, and he could not shake a
basic skepticism that past problems were a long way from being
solved. As Sinyavsky put it, it is "a lot easier to print Boris
Pasternak's novel *Doctor Zhivago* than to produce salami. And if
there's no salami, little by little *glasnost* will die away as well."

Sinyavsky's suspicion that pyramids cannot easily be
transformed into parthenons may well be correct, but in the wake of

the dizzying events of 1989 and 1990, the USSR seems much more to be a house of cards than a pyramid. The economy continues to collapse. The fifteen republics are increasingly asserting their independence and with each passing day the Union of Soviet Socialist Republics seems less likely to survive. Even the Russian republic has declared itself to be sovereign.

Progressive reformers on the republic level have rushed past Gorbachev to seize the initiative on a whole host of economic, political, and human rights fronts. The Eastern European satellite world with its Warsaw Pact now belongs to the pages of history, and Eastern and Western Germany have united on western terms. If there is any lesson to be learned from the fate of this superpower, it is that a house built on sand may look good for a time, but when it begins to collapse it can do so with astounding speed.

It is too early to pronounce with absolute certainty the death of the USSR. Rumors of coups and conservative backlashes abound, and the military and the KGB continue to have frightening power at their disposal. Yet it is difficult to imagine that a Marxist totalitarian superpower can reemerge from the rubble which is engulfing Soviet society.

The early nineties are a time of great ironies. On October 15, 1990, Mikhail Gorbachev was awarded the Nobel Peace Prize. There is probably no foreign leader more respected in the West, and yet at home Gorbachev's popularity is gone and there is virtually no confidence in his reforms. The question is not so much how can the massive blocks of a pyramid be transformed into the soaring columns of the Parthenon, it is what can one build out of a collapsing house of cards?

WILL DEMOCRACY REPLACE COMMUNISM?

Are democracy and communism compatible? That they do not seem to be in the USSR is borne out by recent events, but it is unclear whether it will be full democracy that replaces communism.

If there is any reality the West needs to grasp it is that the demise of communism does not insure the rise of western-style democracy and the full institution of religious freedom, with protection for minority religious groups.

And what is the relationship between socialism and democracy? Gorbachev, like previous Soviet leaders, has often preferred to talk of "socialism" rather than "communism." This has caused considerable confusion in the West, where Scandinavian brands of "socialism" seem harmless.

But it is critical that we sharply distinguish between the "socialism" of Sweden and that which has evolved in the Soviet Union. The former is close to what is generally understood as capitalism, and allows for considerable individual, political, and economic freedom. The latter may call itself "socialist," but it is sufficiently different that we ought to use a different term to describe it. Communism is the traditional term to describe Marxist socialism in action.

Gorbachev seeks to connect the notion that "socialism and democracy are indivisible" with Vladimir Lenin. Western socialism (or rather capitalism with a generous "social net" policy for dealing with the unemployed, the aged, and the disadvantaged) is indeed compatible with democracy, but communism has not yet proven its ability to coexist with democracy.

Gorbachev's hero is a perfect case in point. The general secretary makes no mention in his book on *perestroika* of how Lenin dealt with democracy when he had the opportunity. In the pre-Gorbachev Soviet Union there was only one multi-party national democratic election—a few weeks after the Bolsheviks took power in October 1917. Despite Lenin's strong reservations, the election (which had been scheduled by the Provisional government before the Bolsheviks took over) was held and did not give the Bolsheviks the largest number of delegates.

How did Lenin respond to this disturbing development? On January 4, 1918, the day before the Constituent Assembly was to have its first meeting, Lenin joked: "Since we made the mistake of promising the world that this talk shop would meet, we have to open it up today, but history has not yet said a word about when we will shut it down." When the Constituent Assembly would not go along with what Lenin wanted, he simply refused to let it meet the next day. It was Lenin who abruptly ended the Bolsheviks' one-day experiment with democracy.

So when Gorbachev asserts that for Lenin "socialism and democracy are indivisible," there is some cause for concern. The true test of one's commitment to democracy is whether one allows to stand a people's decision at variance with the Party line.

During most of the first five years of Gorbachev's rule, there was little evidence that the head of the Communist Party would endorse one of the central tenets of Western democracy: the creation of a multiparty political system. What was at stake was the very future and survival of the Communist Party.

In February 1989, Gorbachev told Soviet industrial workers that talk of a multiparty system for the USSR was "rubbish." A few weeks later he told a group of Party leaders from Hungary that what he was trying to create in the Soviet Union was "pluralism within a single-party system." To many democrats in the USSR, this made about as much sense as advocating freedom with chains.

In a remarkable week in April 1989, just a day after an unprecedented Gorbachev-engineered loss of power by almost one-quarter of the Central Committee's more conservative members, a whole series of statements were made demonstrating just how much resistance there still was to genuine democracy. Bemoaning the decline of Party prestige and influence during the Gorbachev years, and the rise of independent political groups and publications, one speaker warned that the nation was in danger of losing its immunity to "ideological AIDS." Though the most strident speeches came from those who were soundly defeated in elections a few weeks before, Gorbachev was as nervous about the proliferation of independent groups as were the conservatives.

On February 10, 1989, a *Pravda* editorial expressed concern about the estimated sixty thousand independent groups which recently had sprung up in the Soviet Union. Among these groups were many which "under cover of democratization, *glasnost,* and national self-assertion" overtly criticize the Soviet system.

The dilemma for Gorbachev is painful. To the extent that full democracy really is important for unleashing the economic and moral resources of a population, interference with its development will only frustrate and impede the ultimate success of *perestroika*. In other words, if democratization is not allowed to develop, *perestroika* will flounder. But if genuine democracy is allowed to evolve, communism as we have known it will cease to exist.

Although Communist revolutionaries have often talked about the "will of the people" and egalitarianism, the record conclusively demonstrates that they do not believe the masses know what is best for them. Marx and Lenin looked down on the vast majority of the population—the peasantry—considering them to be hopelessly conservative or reactionary. It was the proletariat, the urban workers (and even here, only the "socially-conscious" workers) who were slated in theory to lead the revolution. And in the Bolshevik version of Marxist social democracy, a small, elite party was expected to lead. Marxists have never trusted the world's poor to know how to make themselves happy.

In 1978 a Communist party member from Moscow State University explained to me that if the people were given a choice "they would go back to capitalism, and we can't have that." Events in both Eastern Europe and the Soviet Union appear to justify the Party member's fear.

Late in 1989, Gorbachev was still dragging his feet on the question of multiparty democracy. In an article in *Pravda* on November 26, he concluded that "at the present complex stage . . . the difficult tasks of *perestroika* prompt the advisability of keeping the one-party system." But others were pushing ahead to strike at the very heart of the Communist party's legal basis for monopolizing power: Article 6 of the USSR Constitution. This article asserted that the Communist Party was "the guiding force of Soviet society and the nucleus of its political system." In December, Gorbachev argued before the Soviet congress that Article 6 ought not to be put on the agenda. He was opposed particularly by Andrei Sakharov and the Baltic republics, which were already in the process of removing such articles from their own constitutions. Gorbachev's position narrowly won. Within a few days Sakharov was dead, and several weeks later Gorbachev had joined his deceased rival in calling for a multiparty democracy.

In February 1990, the Central Committee plenum recommended abolishing Article 6 of the Soviet Constitution. The next month the Congress of People's deputies endorsed the proposed change. The unheard of had happened: Communist leaders had voted themselves out of the guaranteed driver's seat of the Soviet Union. In February, then ideological chief Vadim Medvedev had argued: "Either we prove able to lead a rapid but controlled process of transformation or it will become an uncontrolled deluge."

But the deluge Medvedev feared could not be stopped, even by significant concessions. At the Twenty-eighth Party Congress in July, Medvedev was not reelected to the Politburo, and Gorbachev's main conservative opponent, Yegor Ligachev, failed in his bid to be elected as deputy general secretary. Gorbachev managed to keep his post as general secretary, garnering three-quarters of the forty-five hundred congress delegate votes cast. A restructured Politburo now guarantees each of the fifteen republics a seat, thus increasing their independence.

The July 1990 congress provided graphic evidence that Gorbachev was failing to stop the breakup of the Communist Party itself. At the very time the congress was meeting, so was the Supreme Soviet of the Russian Republic. Boris Yeltsin, president of the Russian Republic, pointedly chose to spend most of his time presiding over the republic meetings rather than attending the all-union congress sessions. When he did attend it was to denounce the failure of the Communist Party to reform itself or to move quickly enough in setting in motion all-union reforms. Gavril Popov and Anatoly Sobchak (the mayors of Moscow and Leningrad) announced at the congress their intent to leave the Communist Party. Yeltsin soon left the Party as well. On the Sunday after the congress adjourned, a crowd of between 100,000 and 400,000 denounced what the congress had achieved.

In 1989, 136,000 members abandoned the Communist Party. In the first nine months of 1990, an additional 600,000 turned in their Party cards. Throughout 1990, even before the October 9 decision by the Supreme Soviet (or parliament) to grant equal rights to all parties, new parties and party coalitions were cropping up throughout the Soviet Union.

The main issue today is whether there can be a smooth transition to a multiparty democracy in the Soviet Union. The task is made doubly difficult by the immensity of the economic and societal problems that face the peoples of the Soviet Union in the wake of the disastrous experiment with Marxism, and the lack of practical experience in non-totalitarian political arrangements. The initial euphoria following the emergence of the possibility of multiparty politics has now given way to the predictable disharmony and division within and between noncommunist parties.

Between the abdication of the last Russian tsar in February 1917 and the Bolshevik coup of October, Russia experienced almost unlimited *glasnost*, effusive praise of democracy, and the emergence of numerous political powers. Observers of the contemporary Soviet scene who know their history note the striking parallels with today. That earlier period, like its contemporary equivalent, was characterized by a deteriorating economy and a growing sense of insecurity. In the words of an experienced *Izvestiia* columnist in mid-November 1990, "Disappointed by the fruitlessness of democracy, the people are rapidly becoming fertile ground for a 'strong hand.' "

Democracy depends on the art of compromise, on the ability to develop some sort of working relationships with even bitter political foes, and a willingness to bide one's time until the next election if one fails in the present one. In times of chaos and anarchy, the temptation to return to some sort of authoritarian or even totalitarian system will be great.

The degree to which religious freedom and human rights are fully achieved for the peoples of the Soviet Union will directly depend on whether stable democratic institutions can be achieved and democratic habits of the mind and heart cultivated.

THE RISE OF CHRISTIAN DEMOCRATIC GROUPS IN THE USSR

Emerging Christian political activists in the Soviet Union are attracted to the ideals of Christian Democracy, including the assumption that the Christian world view has something significant to offer to the political culture of a society. Soviet activists are also undoubtedly attracted to the strong Christian Democratic record in opposing Marxism as a false and dangerous hope. This is a perspective with which many in the Soviet Union identify, Christian and non-Christian alike.

Alexander Ogorodnikov was the first to attempt the formation of a Christian Democratic movement in the USSR. The Christian Democratic Union of Russia was formed at a conference in Moscow, August 4-7, 1989. According to the founding statutes, "The Christian Democratic Union is a political party, combining Christians of various confessions, whose goal is the spiritual and economic rebirth of Russia and the creation on her territory of a legal democratic government based on the principles of Christian Democracy."

Ogorodnikov's Christian Democratic group has had to deal with a number of external and internal difficulties. Harassment by the authorities, including the suspicious death of Sergei Savchenko, was particularly troubling in the early months. However, there has been internal dissension as well. In April 1990, Keston College reported that four of the CDU leaders had split with Ogorodnikov and were urging that he be defeated for the Moscow City Soviet. Ogorodnikov concedes that there have been problems, but believes they are not unlike those experienced by other Russian political groups. Ogorodnikov was not elected.

A larger, and probably more influential Christian Democratic organization has emerged in the Soviet Union—the Russian Christian Democratic Movement (RCDM). Approximately one hundred people attended an exploratory organizational meeting for the RCDM, which took place in Moscow on March 26, 1990. Father Gleb Yakunin criticized Ogorodnikov's group for "prematurely" founding a "Christian Democratic" group, before there was sufficient backing. A Constitutional Conference was held on April 8-9, and was attended by over three hundred people. In its "Fundamental Principles," the main positions of the new party were set forth:

> Under the rule of the godless regime our country has been brought to the verge of spiritual and physical destruction. For the sake of survival, society must move from an ideology of destruction and hatred to the ideals of constructiveness and solidarity. Only a religious and moral rebirth will open the pathways to beneficial transformations. . . . A renewed Christian community will give Russia new force to restore its historic memory and to create its future.

Though open to Christians of all denominations, the party is predominantly composed of Orthodox believers. A major support community for RCDM is the literary/philosophical journal *Vybor*, edited by Viktor Aksiuchits and Gleb Anishchenko. *Vybor* has spawned a publishing house and a whole series of cultural and educational initiatives. By August 1990, the party claimed already to have about thirty thousand members.

In an interview with *Moscow News*, Viktor Aksiuchits, explained that there were three ideological principles of the new group: anti-communism, Christian faith, and enlightened patriotism. He went on to assert that "West European liberalism could only originate in the bosom of Christianity, which affirms the equality of all people before God. This is the only basis for the development of liberal consciousness and liberal democratic institutions in the West."

Western observers will be confused and then disappointed to learn that there is more than one Christian Democratic party in the Russian republic, but internal divisions are nothing new to Russian politics, even among those who share common enemies. The fact that RCDM is led by individuals who hold prominent positions in the Russian republic parliament and in the Moscow City Council will likely make it a more powerful and popular Christian Democratic organization than Ogorodnikov's, but it is still too early to know for sure.

WILL ECONOMIC *PERESTROIKA* SUCCEED?

In mid-September 1990, the respected British journal *The Economist* concluded that during Gorbachev's first five and a half years in power the Soviet "economy has not merely stood still, it has moved briskly backwards." After an initial growth of 4 percent in the 1986 economy, the rate dropped significantly the next year and was only 1.5 percent in 1988. Living standards not only have failed to improve, but have gotten worse. The rationing of sugar began in Moscow in May 1989. By late October 1990, only twenty basic goods of the government's list of eleven hundred commodities could regularly be found in Soviet stores. In mid-November, Moscow and Leningrad announced plans for full-scale rationing, meaning that Soviet citizens from other cities would not be allowed to buy many products in the two largest and best supplied cities. Nor can the decline be explained away as the painful consequences of instituting necessary, fundamental changes (as has been the case in Poland).

How do we account for this failure? Do the late 1990 economic plans have any chance of being implemented? To answer these questions we must come to terms with what the central issues are and how much more radical the solutions proposed in the 1990s are than those proposed at the beginning of the *glasnost* era.

Consider Gorbachev's perspective as late as 1988 when the updated version of his 1987 book *Perestroika* was published:

> There is the view that [*perestroika*] has been necessitated by the disastrous state of the Soviet economy and that it signifies disenchantment with socialism and a crisis for its ideals and ultimate goals. Nothing could be further from the truth. . . .
>
> Those who hope that we shall move away from the socialist path will be greatly disappointed. Every part of our program of *perestroika*—and the program as a whole, for that matter—is fully based on the principle of more socialism and more democracy.

Or to put it as the skeptical Vladimir Bukovsky does, "Gorbachev does not want to change the system; he wants to save it, together with his skin." If Gorbachev's words were sincere and not motivated by the need to pacify conservatives at home, then *perestroika* on the economic front was doomed from the start.

In sorting through the commentary concerning *perestroika*, the reader invariably runs into a wall of confusion. On the one hand, Gorbachev reported that although the Soviet economy was in considerable trouble and had been stagnating since the late 1970s, *perestroika* was aimed at perfecting socialism, not replacing it.

On the other hand, many Western commentators insisted that the Soviet economy was in terrible shape and its problems were directly tied to its fundamental economic structures. Jean-Francois Revel went so far as to declare that "the socialist economy is everywhere in a state of collapse." (What the French writer has in mind would be better termed "communism.")

An absolutely critical question in all this was whether Gorbachev and the Soviets were willing to face openly the most basic and profound issue of all: Is communism (Marxist-Leninist socialism) itself the core of the problem? Revel gets to the heart of the matter:

> Communist leaders go on affirming that socialism itself remains blameless and all-good. But how is it, then, that from a principle so satisfactory there have evolved nothing but execrable results? Initiatives like Gorbachev's have always been undertaken in the name of the "true" socialism and against the false. Then how is it, again, that even by the testimony of its partisans, there has never been anything but false socialism?

This potentially would lead *glasnost* to a depth that Gorbachev at first showed no willingness to approach.

> And what if the so-called false socialism should turn out to be identical with the true? A terrible question—but real glasnost will not have come about until the contradiction is acknowledged and somehow overcome.

The French newspaper *Le Monde* once summarized Soviet reform efforts and potential as including greatly increasing the autonomy of economic enterprises, revamping management structures nationally, overturning the whole Soviet system of planning, moving toward greater democracy as a means of achieving economic reforms. At one point the French paper asserted: "One cannot minimize the scope of this reform. By every available measure, it is without doubt of the first importance."

The French reporting in question, however, is not about the

On Pyramids, Parthenons, and Houses of Cards   151

second half of the 1980s under Gorbachev. It is about the first few
months of Brezhnev's regime twenty years earlier. To be sure,
Brezhnev did not implement such changes, but it is not unique to talk
about the problems of centralization, lack of incentives, and the need
for basic reforms. Many Soviet leaders have done so, but none have
been willing to use the sharp knife of analysis on their most sacred
beliefs. At least in rhetoric, Gorbachev, too, has sought to keep certain
sacred cows out of the public discussion: Marx, Lenin, socialism, and
communism.

If, to save face, Communist leaders implement capitalist
techniques and simply call them advanced socialism, that is one thing;
but if they do not understand and embrace the empirical advantages of
incentive-driven, market-driven economic forces, and if they play
around the edges at basic changes, the fundamental restructuring so
desperately necessary for economic and social recovery will remain as
elusive as ever. Revel is correct: "The only real way to reform
socialism is to shake free of it. So long as Communist rulers insist on
restructuring the system *in order to save it,* they are on a false trail."
He compares trying to mix socialism and competition with attempts to
drive a boat up a tree or a bicycle across the ocean. Gorbachev
responded to the further downturn of the economy by slowing the
pace of his economic reforms.

A basic question has always been whether Gorbachev has the
desire or the will to make the kind of changes required to revive the
economy. In the 1988 view of the well-known Soviet dissident Yuri
Orlov, "Removing the food deficit and the notorious inefficiency of
both agriculture and industry requires more than the half-measures
currently proposed under *perestroika.* It requires a virtual renunciation
of party control over the economy and a significant expansion of the
scope and influence of the free market."

By 1989 and 1990, in the wake of ever more depressing reports
on the state of the Soviet economy, the folly of "half-measures" was
more and more clear. One attempt to avoid such "half measures" was
the radical proposed program of economics professor Stanislav
Shatalin. He headed an economic planning group which was
instructed to report jointly to Mikhail Gorbachev (as president of the
USSR) and Boris Yeltsin (president of the Russian Republic).
Shatalin's task force struck at two of the central tenets of Marxist
communism—opposition to a market economy and private property.
According to the plan:

Humanity has not yet developed anything more efficient
than a market economy. . . . The prerequisite to ensure the
effective functioning of the market [includes] de jure
equality of all types of property, including private property
. . . revenue from property should be recognized as lawful
profit.

This endorsement of private property was not some theoretical,
rhetorical flourish. The plan called on the central Moscow
government to turn over to the republics the 80 percent of the USSR's
industrial assets which it controlled, and the republics were then to
sell the assets to private entrepreneurs or joint-stock companies.
Collective farms could be divided into private plots. The huge
national budget deficit would be reduced by cutting foreign aid by 75
percent, the military by 10 percent, and the KGB by 20 percent.
Privatization of the Soviet economy was the central feature of the
plan.

Shatalin's so-called "500 Day Program" could have earned him
exile in Siberia or worse just a few years ago, yet on September 11,
1990 the Russian parliament adopted it with just one dissenting vote.
Gorbachev was caught in a dilemma between a more conservative
plan supported by his prime minister, Nikolai Ryzhkov, and the more
radical Shatalin plan supported by Yeltsin. At first he seemed to be
moving towards endorsing the Shatalin plan, but on October 16 he
backed off and came down somewhere between Shatalin and
Ryzhkov. In particular, Gorbachev rejected the "500 day" rapid jump
to a market economy, preferring a more gradual transition.

But even the Gorbachev proposal was a remarkable departure
from Marxism. It endorsed selling state properties to private
individuals or groups (but provided no timetable for its
implementation), allowed collective farms to be privatized, abolished
by the end of 1992 many price controls (except on bread, meat, dairy
products, medicine, and transportation), and shifted much economic
decision-making to the republics. "Freedom of economic activity"
was established as a right. The Gorbachev plan called for sharp cuts
in foreign aid, military, and KGB; and incomplete capital projects
were to be halted. The preamble asserted that "the whole world
experience has proved the vitality and efficiency of the market
economy." The word socialist only appeared once: "the transition to
the market does not contradict the socialist choice of our people."

The Gorbachev plan maintained considerably more central

economic planning than did the Shatalin economic blueprint, and it avoided the rapid privatization of the economy which the more radical Russian republic plan called for. Shatalin conceded that he was not very happy with the Gorbachev plan and did not believe it would lead to a real market economy. Yeltsin attacked the Gorbachev economic blueprint as a tactical retreat which allowed the central government to maintain indefinitely its monopoly on power.

Though by late 1990 Gorbachev had moved a long way toward recognizing just how fundamental the Soviet Union's economic woes were, he still seemed reluctant or unable to avoid "half-measure" solutions.

Meanwhile in the provinces, the demands for radical reforms were becoming much more insistent. A good example is provided in the person of Valery Ryumin. In April 1990, this former military instructor of Marxist-Leninism was elected mayor of Ryazan—a city of over half a million, three hours to the east of Moscow. According to Ryumin, progress depends on breaking the economic stranglehold of feudal-like Party fiefdoms and transferring land ownership to the peasants.

A Soviet joke well illustrates this problem. But first, remember that in Russian, *perestroika* means both "to restructure" and "to rebuild." This gives the joke more punch in the original.

Stalin, Khrushchev, Brezhnev, and Gorbachev all end up outside the Pearly Gates at the same time. Stalin, in a fit of honesty, confesses to St. Peter: "I must admit, I really did not build anything solid during my years as leader." Khrushchev, also overcome by a desire to tell the truth, says, "I, too, did not build anything during my time as general secretary." Brezhnev, without a moment's hesitation, chimes in: "I certainly built nothing." Before Gorbachev can open his mouth, St. Peter turns to him and demands: "Then what in the world did you rebuild?"

Reform is not needed, for that implies something solid to return to; what is needed is revolution. It doesn't matter what the Soviet leaders choose to call it, whether capitalist or socialist. Whatever the name, it had better be closer to what fuels the Western countries than what is behind the failed dream of the Soviet Union since the Bolshevik Revolution. Otherwise, economic breakthroughs can never be realized.

But armchair economic quarterbacks in the West ought to recognize that even if radical steps are finally endorsed and attempted by Gorbachev or a future Soviet leader, this will not guarantee that they will succeed. Seventy years of communism have not only decimated the economy but deprived Soviet society of the kind of freedom which produces and sustains the virtues, talents, and habits necessary to create and sustain a productive economic system. The Soviet peoples are as capable of working as anyone else in the world, but the consequences of many decades without freedom and a collapsing Soviet economy make digging out all the more difficult.

Amidst the chaos and growing anarchy, religious faith may prove an important anchor for many in the Soviet Union. It is, after all, a time-tested source of moral virtue and hope—two vital ingredients to any future economic and societal stability.

Is there a connection between *perestroika* and religious freedom? Definitely. If a strong economic system evolves in the Soviet Union, it will be because the Communist party has decided to allow significant decentralization of the economy. Such a shift will not only break the Party's monopoly on the wealth of the country, but its monopoly on power and ideas as well.

Such a revolutionary move towards pluralism, if buttressed by structural changes in the legal system making it difficult to reassert unitary control, would help create the conditions necessary for religious freedom to flower.

THE FUTURE OF ATHEISM IN THE USSR

If one takes seriously what Karl Marx, Vladimir Lenin, Joseph Stalin, Nikita Khrushchev, and Leonid Brezhnev repeatedly said, atheism is not an optional belief for true communists. It is an absolutely essential tenet of their worldview.

It is essential because a religious orientation fundamentally threatens the classical Marxist notion that human beings are the masters of their own fates and the creators of their own values. In the Soviet context, religion has been a practical threat because to the degree genuine religion existed, there remained an obstacle to absolute state power. Totalitarianism is incompatible with genuinely independent religion.

Certainly the church can be "useful" to a secular Marxist state. It can be a focal point of nationalism and patriotism during war. If properly domesticated and controlled, it can even provide good and sober workers. It can function as a major arm of disinformation, hiding, for example, the degree to which religion is not free. But genuinely independent religion is always a threat to an atheist state.

In order for religious freedom to be secure in the Soviet Union, for the improvements under *glasnost* to have a chance to become permanent, a fundamental and public renunciation of state-sponsored atheism must take place. There must be a commitment to genuine separation of church and state—the church must not dictate policy to the state, nor can the state interfere with the internal affairs of the church. Nor can the state disallow religious involvement in public life. Like any other citizen, a religious citizen must have the right to elect officials and be elected to public office. There must be fundamental, legal, and constitutional guarantees of religious freedom.

If this state of affairs were to come into being, atheistic communism as we have known it would no longer exist. A socialist state, with a wider "social net" even than those currently found in the West, might take its place. But such a state would not represent a threat to religious liberty. It might not function well economically, but its failings would not constrain it to interfere with religious freedom.

A major step toward religious freedom in the USSR occurred in October 1990 with the passage of the Law on the Freedom of Conscience. This legislation disallows further state funding of atheist education, a key ideological mainstay of state-sponsored Marxism. It is much too early, however, to judge whether a full separation of church and state will emerge. Since 1918 and Lenin's declaration of "church/state" and "church/school" separation, there was alleged to be no involvement of the state in church affairs. This was never the case, but in recent years there has been less interference.

The struggle between the ideology of atheism and the existence of religion is much more deadly and basic than the empirical discussion over what works economically. The *perestroika* debate about the latter is not sufficient to deal with the former.

Anyone who thinks that men's minds can be changed simply by making a convincing case regarding the superiority of one form of economic organization over another, has not studied history. The compelling case against collectivized agriculture has been known in the Soviet Union for many years; private plots have long been many times more productive than their collectivist counterparts, yet there has been a systematic refusal by the Party to dismantle collectivization. Ideology is much more powerful than we often imagine. Fidelity to a particular ideology for helping the masses can be much stronger than fidelity to the masses themselves.

When it comes to the struggle between a religious world view and a secular one, more is going on than meets the eye. For the uncommitted person, belief systems are like clothes put on and taken off at will; it doesn't much matter what one wears. But Christians have always believed more was at stake then just a struggle between human beings. As St. Paul expressed it, "our struggle is not against flesh and blood, but against the rulers, against the authorities, against the powers of this dark world and against the spiritual forces of evil in the heavenly realms" (Ephesians 6:12).

To look deep into the well of Christian suffering during the last seventy years in the Soviet Union is not to encounter a "disagreement" between reasonable people about the proper relationship between church and state. It is to come face to face with forces not of the human dimension. Such sentiments are not fashionable in the sophisticated analyses of the present century, but then the evils wrought by Hitler and Stalin soar beyond our pathetic human attempts at comprehension.

This is no simplistic attempt to turn the Soviet Union into an "evil empire," though it has at times been that. Rather, it is a recognition that forces of evil do manifest themselves in a compulsive antireligious form of atheism. You don't argue someone out of such hostility by talking about the benefits to society which a religious person offers. At this level, the hostility springs from one thing and one thing only: a hatred of everything connected with the notion of a sovereign, divine being.

What if Mikhail Gorbachev is not an atheist at all? What if he is, in some sense, a believer? "Preposterous idea!" many will exclaim—but it is a possibility getting some play in the press. Is there any justification for it?

It is well known that Gorbachev's mother is a Russian Orthodox believer, and Gorbachev himself has reported that he was baptized as an infant. His grandparents on his father's side are said to have hidden religious icons behind pictures of Lenin and Stalin hanging on the wall.

According to Mark Helprin in the *Wall Street Journal*, Larry Speakes, press secretary to former President Reagan, comes close to asserting that Gorbachev told Reagan he was a believer. Further evidence that Gorbachev may believe in God is taken from some of his public statements. In 1985, Gorbachev told *Time*, "surely, God on high has not refused to give us enough wisdom to find ways to bring us an improvement in our relations." After beginning his first American visit, Gorbachev commented to former Secretary of State George Shultz: "The visit has begun, so let us hope. May God help us."

Skeptics, of course, have good grounds for suspicion. If Gorbachev is a secret believer, he has had to lie about it in Party circles for decades. Nor can I forget one of Khrushchev's offhand remarks: "Thank God I'm an atheist." The colloquial reference to God in exclamations, whether in the Soviet Union or in the West, tells us little about the speaker's ultimate belief about a divine being.

On the other hand, what Gorbachev truly believes may be considerably more than the skeptics think is possible. And if he is not a doctrinaire atheist, he may be less inclined to moral relativism and belief in the perfectibility of human beings than his classical Marxist predecessors. He seems to have few illusions about how difficult it will be for the Soviet Union to get back on track. "This is the edge of the abyss," Gorbachev commented when describing the strength of his opponents. "One more step and it's the abyss." As Helprin concluded, "Given the correlation of forces, it may be a task fit only for a believer."

Even if it turns out Gorbachev is not a secret believer, Jews and Christians have long believed that in the providence of God, nonbelievers can be used to fulfill God's will. The example of the Persian king Cyrus, who issued the decree for the rebuilding of the temple in Jerusalem (Ezra 1), may offer an interesting parallel to the contemporary Soviet situation. At least such a possibility should not be ruled out.

And even if Gorbachev is neither a closet believer nor a King Cyrus, *perestroika* and *glasnost* have unleashed forces able to challenge the grip of atheism on Soviet society.

THE LANDMINE OF NATIONALISM

An irreconcilable conflict exists between democratization and the maintenance of the Soviet Union as we have known it. The USSR is not a country in the twentieth-century sense of the term; it is an empire made up of many subject nationalities who greatly resent their absorption into the USSR.

The Baltic states were all independent countries between the World Wars; Ukraine has always coveted its fleeting moments of independence; and the Caucasian and Central Asian republics do not appreciate Russian hegemony, either. The problem comes when these groups interpret Gorbachev's rhetoric regarding democratization as a signal to express more independence. Expressions of independence have exploded into demands for autonomy. This is what Gorbachev's critics on the Right have long feared would happen, and it has.

How has Gorbachev responded? It is impossible both to honor the pledge to democratize—to allow the people to decide their own fate—and to continue the empire. If the empire dissolves or breaks apart, religious liberty may expand. If, however, there is a backlash against the expression of non-Russian nationalism, religious liberty in outlying republics may decrease.

But there is another possible scenario. Narrow Russian chauvinists may blame Gorbachev's policies for nationalist unrest. According to Bohdan Bociurkiw, a prominent authority on religion in Ukraine,

> It is not impossible that the threatening disintegration of the Soviet empire may force the Gorbachev regime—in order to counter a conservative Russian nationalist backlash against *glasnost* and *perestroika*—to seek the good will of the so-called "extreme nationalists" supporting Gorbachevite political reforms in Ukraine; should this happen, legalization of the Ukrainian Catholic—on terms analogous to those applied to the Roman Catholic Church in Lithuania—would be a logical concession to West Ukrainians and a policy much more consistent with Gorbachev's stated objectives than the continuation of the Stalinist repression of the Uniates [Ukrainian Catholics].

Indeed, in late 1989 important movement towards legalization of the Ukrainian Catholic church took place.

Some feared that Gorbachev would compromise with Russian nationalists bent on not losing the empire before he would make broad concessions to the nationalities. However, the June 1, 1989 decision of the Congress of People's Deputies to set up a commission of inquiry into the 1940 annexations of the Baltic states was unprecedented and was supported by the general secretary.

What makes the matter so complicated is the mixture of nationalist and religious motivations. In Eastern Europe and in the Soviet Republics, loyalty to the dominant religion of one's native area may genuinely reflect religious conviction, but it is also likely to be a tangible expression of nationalism as well. On the other hand, clamping down on a nationalist religious group may be motivated as much by political considerations as by atheistic ones.

There is no more explosive issue Mikhail Gorbachev must face than that of nationalism. And just as in the issues involving the economy, there is no certainty that Gorbachev knows how to defuse this time bomb. Bohdan Nahaylo's analysis here is instructive.

> Mr. Gorbachev himself now acknowledges that the success of *perestroika* depends on the solution of the national question, but he is still avoiding grappling with the root of the matter. The longer he continues to pretend that harmony would prevail in the "common Soviet fatherland" if not for those "nationalist" trouble-makers, the more serious the national problem is likely to become.

On October 24, 1990, the Supreme Soviets (parliaments) of Russia and Ukraine voted that, except for issues of transport and defense, before all-union Soviet legislation could be implemented in their republics, their legislative approval had to be obtained. Earlier that same day, however, the USSR Supreme Soviet passed its own resolution declaring that all-union laws take precedence over republic laws, thus challenging one of the key provisions included in the numerous republic assertions of sovereignty. It is not clear who will prevail in this power struggle, but the fate of the USSR as we have known it hangs in the balance.

In an address to eleven hundred military officers in Moscow on November 13, Gorbachev pledged to preserve an all-USSR army and a unified economics system. Ominously warning that any attempt to separate people who have "lived side by side for centuries" could "turn into a bloodbath," he went on to assert that an economic breakup of the USSR could spawn a situation even worse than that of the Chinese Cultural Revolution (1966-76) with its chaos and thousands of dead.

Though Gorbachev sought to demonstrate firmness with the military officers, they were not convinced that the Soviet president had matters under control. During the four-hour meeting, officer after officer stood to his feet to express outrage at nationalist extremism, loss of discipline in the military (high desertion rates and draft evasion), economic problems, the "persecution" of Communists, and "one-sided concessions to the West." The next day a deputy to the

USSR Supreme Soviet expressed his growing frustration, arguing that the time had come to choose conclusively between socialism and capitalism. "The people in the factories don't care much which path we choose, as long as they know how they are meant to act. Right now, all we have is chaos. . . . Let the president make up his mind."

CONCLUSION

Before full religious freedom can be secured for the peoples of the USSR, antireligious ideology must be publicly and firmly renounced as incompatible with a progressive, socially just, modern Soviet State. Outlawing state-sponsored atheism is a crucial step towards religious freedom. If this new legal prohibition is enforced, the ideological age of Soviet atheism will have ended. But the fate of religious groups in the USSR will also be greatly affected by the political and economic drama now unfolding in this troubled empire.

A number of serious issues will have to be resolved before *glasnost* and *perestroika* become permanent features on the Soviet landscape. Democratic institutions must be allowed to undermine the power base of the Communist party and to set up institutional and structural guarantees protecting inalienable human rights. Economic rethinking must be allowed to question the fundamentals of Marxist and Communist economic creeds, and fresh ideas must be given an opportunity to unleash the creativity and power of the Soviet people.

The continuation of *glasnost* and *perestroika* depends in part on granting the non-Russian republics either independence or meaningful autonomy within a truly federal system. If this does not occur, then religious freedom (to say nothing of political freedom) of non-Russians will be in great jeopardy.

CHAPTER 9

A CHRISTIAN RESPONSE
TO *GLASNOST*

*I*n the Vatican hangs a well-known sixteenth-century painting by Raphael titled *School of Athens*. The work depicts both the "other world" and "this world" sides of Greek philosophy. Plato stands pointing to the heavens, while the practical Aristotle gestures toward the earth as if cautioning those present not to forget the ground on which they stand.

It is that sort of "both/and" attitude that Christians ought to have about recent developments in the Soviet Union. It is a time to utilize fully both our hearts and our heads. It is a time both to rejoice and to be sober. To do either to the exclusion of the other is to misunderstand badly the dynamic of this moment—and in so doing, fail to understand the opportunities to be grasped.

On the one hand, there are tangible signs of positive change for believers: releases from labor camp and exile; greater availability of religious literature; the opportunity to contribute to society in the form of charity; wonderful, new possibilities for evangelization; the possibility of legally organizing religious education for children; a new, more open and positive attitude toward religion in the Soviet press and literature; more liberal laws and regulations dealing with religious organizations; and a generally more lenient attitude toward believers by the authorities.

On the other hand, problems remain. That the laws governing religious groups have been significantly liberalized ought not blind us to the fact that the Soviet state seeks to register religious groups.

Why should they do so? Also, juridical statutes on the rights of believers will not be secure until they exist within a genuinely democratic context—that is, one which has real political checks and balances and separation of powers. The Soviet Union need not emulate Western forms of democracy, but it will have to find a way to obtain the essential feature: a genuine dispersal of power among the people and among the diverse non-governmental groups within Soviet society.

Practice has yet to conform fully with rhetoric. Many Soviet commentators have acknowledged this. Throughout the Gorbachev era there have been many accounts of continued problems: fines and short jail sentences for holding unregistered religious gatherings, as well as longer sentences for refusing to serve in the military; interference with the reception, printing, and spread of religious literature; and a continuing harassment of some unregistered religious activities. To be sure, these problems have been less serious than in the past. But for certain groups and in certain parts of the USSR, the warm winds of *glasnost* have yet to melt fully the icy past.

Western experts on the Soviet Union, including many religious ones, are quick to point out some of the more obvious reasons for the changes. Kremlin pragmatists recognize that a more open society is necessary to revitalize a stagnant economy. Antireligious activities are unnecessary, waste state resources, fail to utilize fully some of the best workers in the Soviet Union, and irritate Western world opinion at a time when the USSR needs foreign investment and good will. Religious believers in the Soviet Union are needed: They provide a model of moral life—good marriages, honesty, and a means of dealing with drug and alcohol problems.

But while we analyze these changes in the Soviet Union and ponder the likely economic and political causes of a more liberal environment, we run the risk of missing a key point. As one Canadian evangelist has put it: "God is behind *glasnost* and *perestroika*. The people in the Soviet Union are waking up from the opiate of atheism and are turning to God."

Although we ought not to declare a full-fledged religious revival in the USSR, the signs of response by the Soviet people to the gospel are unmistakable. In religious terms, *glasnost* must be understood, in part, as "repentance." Indeed, that is the title of the major *glasnost*-era Soviet film.

In the fall of 1988, in the city of Rostov on the Don River in southern Russia, a man approached an evangelist and pleaded for forgiveness. The preacher, Joseph Bondarenko, did not understand what the man was talking about. Then the stranger reached into his pocket and pulled out his KGB identification: "I am the one who put you behind bars. Please forgive me!"

At another service, a young man came forward, accepted Christ, then turned to the congregation and made the following remarkable statement: "I am the editor of an atheist paper. People, I have been deceiving you. Please forgive me. God is real!"

It should be obvious that millions of Soviet citizens—reared in an atheist country, unconnected to the church and without religious convictions—remain unaware and untouched by the several thousand recent conversions. But that is how it has always been in the history of the church. A committed minority comes to believe and in turn becomes the catalyst for much larger groups coming to know and accept Christian truths.

Even among atheists who show no interest in converting, there is noticeable irritation and boredom with the clumsiness and narrowness of atheism, particularly in its militant forms. Atheist Marxism has had many decades to create a cohesive, committed, "new" society. It has utterly failed to do so. Nationalism is a much more powerful force in all its manifestations than the idea of communism.

But nationalism, particularly non-Russian nationalism, is precisely what may spell the greatest political danger for the continuation of Gorbachev's reforms. Will Gorbachev permit the dismantling of the Soviet empire? But that is what hundreds of thousands, perhaps millions, of Soviet citizens want in the Baltic states, Ukraine, Georgia, and other republics. They believe Gorbachev's rhetoric of "democratization" must mean "self-determination," or else it is just another version of the worn-out propaganda of the past.

The other reality which could spell defeat for Gorbachev is economic. If he fails to grasp how fundamental the economic changes must be (that is, that basic Marxist-Leninist assumptions must be challenged), then economic *perestroika* will not produce enough tangible economic benefits to maintain a support base among the people.

Gorbachev is seeking economic successes which strengthen the country internally, enhance its reputation internationally, and enjoy the enthusiastic support of the population. On the other hand, those who are nervous about his reforms are looking for pretexts to use against him. Nationalist unrest and economic failure provide valuable ammunition for Gorbachev's enemies.

Perhaps Gorbachev can work out something with the constituent republics short of total independence, yet involving greater autonomy—a kind of genuinely federal system. And perhaps he understands, or will come to understand, how radical the economic changes must be if he is to unleash the economy. And perhaps Gorbachev, through careful control of political appointments and clever internal alliances, can hold on to power during difficult years when there may be little to show for his policies.

Perhaps. But the West must neither underestimate the obstacles ahead nor rule out the possibility they can be hurdled. Western analysts would be well advised to understand the cyclical nature of Soviet history and the powerful forces which must be neutralized before it can break free.

The Soviet Union today is something like a spaceship circling the earth. From time to time it fires its engines in an attempt to develop sufficient thrust to escape the gravitational pull of earth. But though it occasionally ventures out a few miles beyond its normal orbit, it has invariably been drawn back toward the ground.

The challenge of *glasnost* and *perestroika*, from a political and economic standpoint, is to find the power necessary to break out of the orbit of stagnation and repression endemic to Marxist, atheist communism. Part of the tension of the present is that Soviet leadership either will not or cannot fully acknowledge the connection between breaking out of its problems and abandoning the ideological commitments of the past.

The world watches as this dramatic experiment in political and economic liberalization takes place. The final outcome is not known, but a complete return to the past is almost inconceivable. Even should the forces of reaction win out, they will likely be unable to put the genie back in the bottle.

Soviet power has historically rested on two things: the control of the military and the control of information. Of the two, the latter is at least as dangerous as the former. In recent months there has been an explosion of information illuminating "blank spots" in Soviet history, and "blank spots," once filled in, cannot be made blank again. The historical memory of the Soviet people has been publicly and forever altered, and it is beyond the power of the Communist party to restore the earlier picture.

Every day that passes with more information on the loose is a further guarantee that there cannot be a full return to the way things were. That does not mean there cannot be a reaction of considerable proportions; there can. The Soviet people are used to such reversals, and that is why they are considerably more temperate than we in the West when asked to predict the future of *glasnost*.

ADVICE FOR WESTERN CHRISTIANS

In light of the preceding analysis, how ought Western believers respond to this critical moment in Soviet history?

1. We must celebrate the power of God to sustain his people in the Soviet Union for more than seventy years under incredibly difficult circumstances.

Even before *glasnost* the church was alive and vibrant, though significantly decreased in size from its pre-Soviet period. Its resiliency was part of what compelled authorities to realize that apart from physically exterminating every believer, there would be no way to rid society of the church. It is true that parts of the church have been badly compromised; but even where compromise appears to be the greatest, there are remarkable signs of life. And where compromise failed to gain a foothold, a fresh group of martyrs has gone forth to join those of other times and other places to provide models of faithfulness for future generations.

2. We ought to acknowledge fully the positive changes which have occurred and are occurring.

It is dishonest and counterproductive to allow the bitterness of the past to blind us to the very real changes of *glasnost*. Though a few in the Soviet Union may see the present changes as little more than a pragmatic necessity until communism can regain its balance, most others genuinely desire a more free and open society, a society which has no need to persecute or discriminate against religion.

3. We must firmly resist the temptation to enfold ourselves in the euphoria of the present while denying the major problems which remain.

So long as one prisoner is confined for his or her religious commitments, so long as believers are not allowed the full rights of other citizens, so long as full religious freedom is denied, so long as talk is limited to "revising" rather than "abolishing" laws regulating religious communities, there is much left to do. So long as the four-million-strong Ukrainian Catholic church is still prevented from obtaining complete freedom and access to all its churches, there is cause for protest.

We must never forget that rhetoric is not reality, though it can be an important first step toward achieving it. Those who respond to every statement of the Soviets with a long list of broken promises are only half-correct. Their warnings ought to serve as a check on the many Westerners dazzled by promises of change. But skeptics must understand that much being said by Soviet authorities today would never have been said in the past. It is extremely dangerous to make sweeping statements that, in the court of world opinion, may one day prove to be lies. To be shown a liar is much more humiliating than never to have made the promises at all.

Thus, while we must be sober and measure words by deeds, we must realize that words can be an important first step to actions. It is a time to use our heads, not our hearts or our desires. We must do our homework and let the chips fall where they may.

4. Now, more than ever, we must fully support those research institutions which have a track record of providing accurate information on religion in Communist countries.

Places like Keston College in England and the dozens of responsible parachurch mission and information groups which provide millions of people with reliable information deserve our generous support.

The focus of many such groups has already shifted dramatically from the plight of prisoners and their families to describing the remaining problems and the unique opportunities of the present. Resources are being redirected to help in tangible ways Christians in the Soviet Union who are starved for religious literature and contact with their co-religionists abroad.

It would be a major tragedy if Western support for these missions and information groups faded precisely at the moment when they are most needed. It would be like returning a kickoff ninety-five yards, then walking off the field five yards short of the goal line. The opportunities available today are unprecedented. Research institutions like Keston College can provide the roadmap, the guidebook, to what help can be given, and yet support for Keston has been steadily eroding since Gorbachev came to power.

5. We must respond generously and quickly to the opportunities now available for helping fellow Christians in the Soviet Union.

While many groups have permission from the Soviet Union to supply large quantities of Bibles, commentaries, and other religious materials, they often do not have sufficient funds to print these materials. Christian churches in the Soviet Union have requested and need tape recorders, video equipment, tapes (recorded and blank), and other supplies which would help their ministries. Much of this can be mailed or shipped in under existing Soviet laws.

Given the personal and church resources of Western Christians, it would be irresponsible not to respond to these opportunities with great generosity. Churches and individuals could include in their missions budget groups like Keston College, Slavic Gospel Association, Open Doors, the United Bible Societies, and many other fine groups which are working hard to meet these unique needs.

There is no guarantee that the present opportunities will long exist. Even if they do last for some time, the possibility of sharing the gospel, of nurturing the church, is not something we can delay even for a single day. The budgets of the parachurch mission groups—and one would hope the church mission groups—ought to expand dramatically in the coming months.

We must provide assistance in direct consultations with Christians in the USSR. Only in this way can we truly meet their needs.

We Western Christians do not render help because we are spiritually superior, but because we have it within our power to meet real needs. We must pray that out of the vitality of the Soviet church may come a revival that in turn will touch off a religious reawakening in the Western church. We, too, exist in a secular society, and our churches are often anemic and apathetic. How many of us would have been faithful had the price of our faith been the persecution and discrimination suffered by fellow believers in the Soviet Union? Most of us would not have mustered the strength to become a member of a registered church, let alone an unregistered one.

6. We need to expand dramatically our written and personal contact with fellow believers in the Soviet Union.

Never have the opportunities for such contacts been greater. Believers from the West ought to travel to the USSR and bring religious literature and other supplies when they go. This can be done legally. In addition to supplying Christians with desperately needed and wanted literature and materials, the fellowship between believers will tremendously help and inspire all concerned. We have much to learn from the vitality and vibrancy of Christians in the Soviet Union.

We must broaden our vision of evangelism beyond crusades and sermons to include diverse contacts of all sorts: lawyer to lawyer, doctor to doctor, professor to professor, politician to politician, and student to student. The opportunities for Christian leaders and professionals to interact with their often secular counterparts are significant. What is needed is imagination and boldness on our part.

7. We need a new commitment to long-term missions.

Many Christians are ready to jump on the first plane to Moscow. This is often not the best thing to do. The present dynamic historical moment ought not to be exploited as a photo opportunity for ourselves, our friends, or our organizations. It is natural to want to be present when the walls crumble, but there must be many who take the long view.

We need Christian young people who are open to the call of God on their lives to long years of language study and becoming *thoroughly* grounded in the history and culture of the peoples of the USSR and Eastern Europe. For every one hundred who responded earlier to the excitement of smuggling Bibles into the USSR, or who will now enthusiastically plan a quick trip to the Soviet Union, one will be willing to submit to tedious and demanding study. Yet the richest harvest in the long term will be the fruit of unglamorous and lengthy study. We must pray that many will pursue language study and graduate study as their special calling. There will be many mission opportunities for such prepared and dedicated individuals.

8. We must reassess critically our past contacts with believers in the Soviet Union.

Too often in the past, the Western church—from ecumenical church organizations right through to evangelicals—has played directly into the hands of the architects of Soviet disinformation. This was surely one of the great Soviet foreign policy successes from the early 1960s on. The Soviets succeeded in silencing Western Christian leaders in ways far exceeding what they were able to accomplish with Western Jews, psychiatrists, scientists, literary figures, and political leaders.

Why did so many Western Christians fail to portray accurately the plight of believers in the Soviet Union? Their motives varied. Some appear to have believed what they were told by Soviet and church authorities. Others believed only part of what they were told, but incorrectly assumed that speaking out about problems would endanger their co-religionists in the Soviet Union. Others were more attracted to the foreign policy agenda of the Kremlin than to that of the White House, or their fear of nuclear war kept them silent on human rights violations in Communist countries. Still others maintained silence because they believed this to be the price for opportunities to evangelize Communist areas.

Some Western believers overreacted to this silence and inaccurate reporting by focusing exclusively, and sometimes sensationally or inaccurately, on the plight of the persecuted. It was good, of course, that those ignored or neglected by Western religious leaders should be defended; but it was unfair that any Soviet Christian who was part of the registered church world should be vilified. While it is true that registered church leaders frequently misrepresented their situation, it should have been recognized that the situation was exceedingly complex, involving a full spectrum of appropriate and inappropriate church actions.

There have always been those across denominational lines who have understood the unique problems and challenges of both the registered and the unregistered churches. There have always been those who were willing, in the same speech, to talk favorably about both groups, about those who felt they must make concessions to the authorities and those who believed they could not. There have always been those who believed it was possible to maintain contacts with both registered and nonregistered, to utilize both public and silent diplomacy in the defense of believers in the USSR. There have always been such people—but there have been far too few, and the views and politics of less balanced approaches have too often set the agenda.

9. We must defuse interdenominational tension.

What a tragedy it would be if the oppression of the Communists were replaced by religious discrimination of one religious group by another. Prior to the arrival of communism in Eastern Europe and the Soviet Union, it was not uncommon for an established state church to actively encouraged discrimination against other Christian groups and other religions. The Orthodox mistreated Protestants in the Russian Empire, while Protestants and Catholics sometimes mistreated minority religious groups in other countries or regions. The Orthodox believe they are mistreated today in the Western Ukraine where the Catholics are in the majority, while the Ukrainian Catholics remember decades of mistreatment at the hands of the Orthodox. The tension between Catholics and Protestants in Northern Ireland is another example of fierce and bitter rivalry. The point is not to draw up a balance sheet of all the injustices suffered by one religious group at the hands of another, but rather to note that interreligious and interdenominational tensions are a poignant fact of life in the Soviet Union which must not be side-stepped. Some suggestions for improving interdenominational relations include the following.

First, Protestant evangelism efforts in the Soviet Union need to be extremely sensitive to Orthodox culture and concerns. The most important religious influence on Russian history is Orthodoxy, and not to understand well the Orthodox faith is to be deprived of a key ingredient for coming to terms with the Russian soul. Orthodox theology and worship are profoundly important and precious jewels within the history of Christianity. Protestants need to be aware of this tradition for the sake of their own enrichment, as well as to be better equipped for ministry within a context shaped largely by Orthodoxy.

Second, any proposal to resurrect a state or established church ought to be firmly resisted. This goes for establishing Orthodoxy as the state religion in Russia, or Catholicism in Lithuania or Ukraine, or particular Protestant denominations elsewhere in the world. This is both to protect the rights of religious minorities and to encourage the vitality of all the religious groups. Both majority and minority religious groups tend to be stronger when they must depend on themselves, and not on state subsidies, to do their basic work. This does not preclude the possibility, even likelihood, that a state will decide that it is in a society's best interests to encourage religious groups in various ways. The issue here is whether it is wise to give preferential treatment to any particular religious group. It is not.

Third, Christians and human rights advocates in the West, in cooperation with like-minded people in the Soviet Union, ought to work for the establishment of legal guarantees protecting religious freedom and the rights of all religious groups regardless of size.

Fourth, Christians in the West, in cooperation with like-minded Christians in the Soviet Union, ought to work for an atmosphere within the Christian community which allows, even encourages, missionary activity from a variety of traditions. The decades of atheist indoctrination, the deprivation of contact with religious teaching—Orthodox or otherwise—has been so damaging that this is not the time to divide the Soviet Union into denominational folds, with keep-out signs posted against different Christian groups. There is plenty of work for all to do and the grace of God is not limited to any one religious group. There ought to be a sweet spirit of fellowship, or at least respectful tolerance, between Christians of different traditions, even when there are major differences on certain doctrinal points. What we have in common ought to be more important than what divides us.

A CALL FOR WESTERN CHRISTIAN UNITY

One consequence of our fallen humanity is that we find it exceedingly difficult to heal past divisions between Christian brothers and sisters.

This is the case in the Soviet Union no less than in the West. Divisions between the registered and the unregistered, between the Russian Orthodox hierarchy and dissidents within that church, are deep, frequently bitter, and cultivated by Soviet authorities. We ought not to be too quick to judge. The unregistered have felt, quite rightly, that they have often been betrayed and abandoned by their registered counterparts. On the other hand, the registered have frequently felt, quite rightly, slandered and misrepresented by the unregistered. As one registered Baptist told me, "God put Daniel in the lion's den, but he didn't ask him to pull the lion's tail." Time and God will have to sort out the truth on both sides, and I suspect there will prove to be saints (and villains) in both camps.

Part of the healing in the Soviet church for which we must pray is that forgiveness and reconciliation can restore unity to the Body of Christ.

In the West, we too have our battle scars, and feelings often run deep. Those who believe the conduct of Western religious leaders toward believers in the USSR has been inadequate (and even shameful) have been swift to label such leaders as unwitting accomplices of Communist propaganda. On the other side, those who have confined themselves to the registered world have too often dismissed as political pawns of anti-Communist Western ideology those who have talked more forthrightly about religious repression in the Soviet Union. Goodwill is not often encountered under such circumstances.

But as raw and sensitive as all of our egos are, as inclined as each of us is to defend ourselves against unjust and perceived unjust attacks, we must work to put aside our differences and seek a new unity in Christ. As strong as the temptation is to settle old political and religious scores, the opportunities of the present and the call of God compel us to work together in common cause.

There are fine, reflective, and sensitive Christians in all Western Christian groups and denominations who are willing to join hands in seeking more effective ways to help our fellow Christians in the USSR. Yes, we do need to deal with the "blank spots" of our own history, our own failings—but more importantly, we need to commit together to do better in the future. We need to do this for two reasons.

First, millions of dollars need to be raised quickly to take advantage of current opportunities. We all hope the doors remain open, but the situation is unstable and the future uncertain.

Second, we must learn from our mistakes so that if *glasnost* does end and a new period of persecution and discrimination begins, we will be a more effective and coordinated Christian community working on behalf of those who suffer. Learning these lessons will serve us well in dealing with all Communist countries—indeed, in dealing with all countries lacking full religious freedom.

CONCLUSION

Westminster Abbey's contribution to the millennium celebrations of the Soviet Union was the world premiere of a new choral work on November 21, 1988. But this was no ordinary performance.

The forty-four-year-old British composer, John Tavener, was himself a convert to Russian Orthodoxy. His work, "Akathist of Thanksgiving," was based on a poem written by Archpriest Grigory Petrov shortly before his death in a Siberian prison camp. Some of Father Petrov's last words are contained in Tavener's hymn of gratitude:

> What is my praise before you? I have not heard the cherubim singing, that is the lot of souls sublime, but I know how nature praises you. In winter I have thought about the whole earth praying quietly to you in the silence of the moon, wrapped around in a mantle of white, sparkling with

diamonds of snow. I have seen how the rising sun rejoiced in you, and choirs of birds sang forth glory. I have heard how secretly the forest noises you abroad, how the winds sing, the waters gurgle, how choirs of stars preach of you in serried motion through unending space.

There is no more poignant testimony to the difference between Marxism and Christianity than that a Christian martyr would end his earthly existence in a spirit of praise to God rather than in bitterness towards his oppressor. English writer G.K. Chesterton has observed that the origin of theology is gratitude.

Soviet television was on hand to film the final rehearsal, and many members of the Soviet Embassy in London were present for the performance.

For the sake of all Soviet citizens, we must pray that their leaders come to understand fully the truth of Gleb Yakunin's words:

Religion is like salt which protects humanity from decomposition and disintegration. Any attempt to banish it from social life invariably leads to a degradation of society.

The success of *glasnost* and *perestroika* will depend largely on Soviet leaders coming to terms with the practical consequences of recognizing the fundamental inalienability of religious freedom.

But far more important for the Christian community is what it believes about the faithfulness and ultimate victory of God over anything this world can assemble against his existence or that of his people. As St. Paul put it in Romans 8:35-39:

Who shall separate us from the love of Christ? Shall trouble or hardship or persecution or famine or nakedness or danger or sword? As it is written: "For your sake we face death all day long; we are considered as sheep to be slaughtered." No, in all these things we are more than conquerors through him who loved us. For I am convinced that neither death nor life, neither angels nor demons, neither the present nor the future, nor any powers, neither height nor depth, nor anything else in all creation, will be able to separate us from the love of God that is in Christ Jesus our Lord.

In the final analysis, the fate of Christians in the Soviet Union depends on God, not Gorbachev or *glasnost*. But in the providence of God, *glasnost* may represent the crude, punched-out windows through which the fresh winds of religious truth may blow into the stale confines of a narrow ideological prison.

May our thankfulness be expressed in deeds, for it is in that unique combination of divine providence and human response that the will of God is done on this earth.

APPENDIX
WHAT WESTERN CHRISTIANS
CAN DO TO HELP

Never during the Soviet period have the opportunities been as great for Christians in the West to help their co-believers in the USSR. This appendix is a resource guide for responding to this unique open door.

There is a serious shortage of religious literature in the Soviet Union. In addition to a tremendous demand for more Bibles in many languages, there is a great need for theological works, training materials for preparing ministers and priests, and religious literature for children. Church ministries could also be aided considerably by many more video players, video tapes, audio cassettes, computers, and religious goods.

An excellent resource on parachurch organizations involved in ministry to countries of Eastern Europe and the USSR is Mark Elliott's *East European Missions Directory* (1989, 81 pages), available from the Institute for East-West Christian Studies ($25 with postage; address listed later in appendix). Elliott has identified over 185 public missions, 56 broadcasters, and 35 research, education, and public advocacy groups.

Space limitations allow me to list only a few of the many fine organizations that provide information on or are working in the Soviet Union. There are more Protestant than Catholic or Orthodox groups involved in supplying literature, but I have tried to identify the non-Protestant groups in parentheses whenever possible so members of those faith communities will know who to contact. (Many of the

Protestant groups distributing Bibles provide them to non-Protestants as well.)

COORDINATING CHRISTIAN MINISTRIES IN THE SOVIET UNION

The explosion of opportunities and interest in Christian ministry to the Soviet Union has created an urgent need for the creation of a clearinghouse of information on opportunities, organization programs, and personnel available for long-term and short-term assignment. As a result of initial funding from World Vision and the Institute on Religion and Democracy, the USSR Christian Resource Center was founded in the spring of 1991 in Washington, D.C. For further information, contact:

Kent R. Hill
USSR Christian Resource Center
1331 H Street N.W., Suite 900
Washington, DC 20005

Also administratively located at the offices of the Institute on Religion and Democracy is the Coalition for Solidarity with Christians in the USSR. Founded in 1987, this interdenominational coalition of twenty-seven organizations seeks to promote cooperation and an exchange of information between groups. When necessary, the Coalition intercedes on behalf of Christians who are experiencing discrimination or persecution.

During 1991, the Lausanne Committee for World Evangelization launched a project titled "Eastern Europe/U.S.S.R. Strategy Study." The purpose is to discover and publicize to churches and Christian organizations ways in which they may help send Christian resources and Scriptures to Eastern Europe and USSR. For further information, contact:

Tom Houston
LCWE
P.O. Box 300
Oxford OX2 9XB
United Kingdom
Tel: 011-44-865-749-070

RESEARCH ORGANIZATIONS

Keston College
Keston Research
33a Canal Street
Oxford, OX2 6BQ
United Kingdom
Tel: 011-44-865-311-022

Keston, USA
P.O. Box 1310
Framingham, MA 01701

General Director: Rev. Canon Michael Bourdeaux

Keston, USA is the American affiliate of Keston College in England, the foremost organization in the world for the study of religion in Communist countries. Keston was founded in 1969 by Michael Bourdeaux. It provides up-to-date information through *Keston News Service* (biweekly, $50 per year), *Keston FAX* ($125 per year), *Religion in Communist Lands* (quarterly, $30 per year, *Frontier* (bimonthly popular magazine, $15 per year), and the publication of books.

Institute for East-West Christian Studies Wheaton College
Wheaton, IL 60187-5593
(708) 260-591

Director: Dr. Mark R. Elliott

The Institute for East-West Christian Studies assists Christian workers, scholars, and the Soviet Union and Central and Eastern Europe. In addition, the East-West Intitute engages in research and facilitates Christian ministry in the Soviet Union and Central and Eastern Europe. The Institute realizes its mission through the acquisition, production, and dissemination of a wide range of resources and through sponsorship of various educational and inspirational forums.

Research Center for Religion and
Human Rights in Closed Societies
475 Riverside Drive
New York, NY 10115
(212) 870-2481 or 2440

Executive Director: Olga Hruby

Established in 1962, the Center holds conferences and publishes information, including its quarterly journal, *Religion in Communist Dominated Areas* (RCDA, $25 per year).

RELIGIOUS LITERATURE

In recent years, the Soviets have been allowing numerous packages of religious literature and other goods to reach their destinations by mail or in large shipments. Bibles and other religious literature may be obtained from the following organizations. If an individual sends in materials, it is best to send no more than three books in one package, preferably of different titles. Most will prefer simply to make a contribution to an organization.

Slavic Gospel Association
P.O. Box 1122
Wheaton, IL 60189
(708) 690-8900

American Bible Society
1865 Broadway
New York, NY 10023
(212) 408-1499

Open Doors/USA
P.O. Box 27001
Santa Ana, CA 92799
(714) 531-6000

Door of Hope International
P.O. Box 303
Glendale, CA 91209
(818) 956-7500

Light in the East
39 Pilgrim Way
Westburg, NY 11590
(516) 334-6792

Inst. for Bible Translation
Box 20100
S-10460 Stockholm
Sweden
Tel: 08-94-5414

World Bible Translation Ctr.
P.O. Box 820648
Fort Worth, TX 76182
(817) 595-1664

Religious Books for Russia
P.O. Box 522
Glen Cove, NY 11542
(Orthodox)

Bibles for the World
P.O. Box 505
Wheaton, IL 60189
(708) 668-7733

International Bible Society
P.O. Box 62970
Colorado Springs, CO 80962
(719) 488-9200

Eastern European Bible Mission
P.O. Box 110
Colorado Springs, CO 80901
(719) 577-4450

OTHER MISSION AND SERVICE MINISTRIES

Many of the groups listed above, such as Slavic Gospel Association, are also involved in religious education, evangelism, and in providing a wide variety of material resources needed by Christians and churches in the Soviet Union. Organizations which specialize in ministries that go beyond Bible distribution include:

Aid to the Church in Need
P.O. Box 576
Deer Park, NY 11729-0576
(Catholic)

Rise Foundation
7424 Piney Branch Road
Tacoma Park, MD 20912
(Orthodox)

Issachar Frontier
Mission Strategies
19321 44th Ave. West, #204
Lynnwood, WA 98036
(206) 744-0400

Youth with a Mission
(Slavic Ministries)
P.O. Box 4213
Salem, OR 97302
(503) 363-1571

Operation Mobilization
P.O. Box 2277
Peachtree, GA 30269
(404) 631-0432

Mission Possible
P.O. Box 2014
Denton, TX 76202
(817) 382-1508

Christian Solidarity Int'l.
P.O. Box 70563
Washington, DC 20024
(301) 989-0298

Logos Bible Training
by Extension
P.O. Box 409
Fresno, CA 93708-0409
(209) 291-6874

Lithuanian Catholic Religious Aid
351 Highland Boulevard
Brooklyn, NY 11207
(718) 647-2434

RADIO BROADCASTERS

One of the most effective ways of helping Christians in the Soviet Union during the past difficult decades has been radio broadcasting. But the importance of radio is no less great today; in fact, the opportunities for the effective use of broadcasting have never been greater. These ministries depend heavily on the support of individual Christians and churches. There is much more that could be done if only the support were available to expand these vital ministries. Some of the better known broadcasters include:

International Russian Radio/TV
Box 225414
Dallas, TX 75222
(817) 354-8110

IBRT
Hannu Haukka
Box 71
04251 Kerava
Finland
(358) 0-2945400

Slavic Gospel Association
Nick Leonovich
P.O. Box 1122
Wheaton, IL 60189
(708) 690-8900

Russian Christian Radio
P.O. Box 1667
1732 Mountain View Court
Estes Park, CO 80517
(303) 586-8638

Far East Broadcasting Co.
Box 1
La Mirada, CA 90637
(213) 947-4651

Trans World Radio
International Headquarters
Box 700
Cary, NC 27512-0700
(919) 460-9596

Radio Vatican
00120
Vatican City
Italy

Holy Archangel Broadcasting
Center (Orthodox)
3770 39th Street NW
Washington, DC 20016
(202) 363-1602

Mennonite Brethren Communications
Victor Hamm
Box 2, Station F
Winnipeg, Manitoba R2L 2A5
Canada
(204) 667-9576

Voice of Orthodoxy
P.O. Box 501
Tuckahoe, NY 10707

EXCHANGES/CONTACTS

Christian Academic/Cultural.
A number of colleges and seminaries are now engaged in or have

conducted exchanges with Soviet institutions. The Christian College Coalition, representing approximately eighty institutions of higher education, would be a good source of information on opportunities which exist. Contact:

John Bernbaum
Vice President
Christian College Coalition
329 8th Street NE
Washington, DC 20002
(202) 546-3086

The International Institute for Christian Studies is establishing departments of Christian studies at secular educational institutions in Eastern Europe and the USSR. Western Christian faculty who are interested in teaching in such a department can contact:

Daryl McCarthy
Executive Director
International Institute for Christian Studies
Box 13157
Overland Park, KS 66212
(913) 339-6530

Campus Crusade for Christ, International Teams/USA, and InterVarsity are involved in setting up academic/cultural exchanges or contacts. Contact:

Glen Tosaya
Campus Crusade for Christ
P.O. Box 62245
Colorado Springs, CO 80962
(719) 593-0300

Mark K. Dyer
International Teams/USA
P.O. Box 203
Prospect Heights, IL 60070
(708) 870-3800

Chuck Ellis
Inter-Varsity Christian Fellowship
6400 Schroeder Road
P.O. Box 7895
Madison, WI 53707-7895
(608) 274-9001

Professional and Miscellaneous Contacts. Much of Soviet

Madison, WI 53707-7895
(608) 274-9001

Professional and Miscellaneous Contacts. Much of Soviet
society no longer identifies itself with religious belief, though it is
open to contacts with Christians. The present situation is ideal for
Western Christians to explore avenues of contact with their
professional counterparts in the Soviet Union.

HELPING SOVIET CHRISTIANS WHO LEAVE THE USSR

Sponsor a Refugee Family.
World Relief is the international humanitarian assistance arm of
the National Association of Evangelicals. While there are ten national
organizations contracted to sponsor and resettle refugees, World
Relief is the only organization responsible for working primarily with
the evangelical Christian denominations in resettling refugees in the
United States.

The chief objective of the sponsor is to help the refugee to
integrate quickly and successfully into American society. The
responsibilities of sponsoring a family include meeting their initial
material needs (housing, clothing, food) as well as their spiritual and
emotional needs (adjusting to the Western church, for example). If
your church or community is interested in getting involved in a direct
ministry to aid Soviet refugees, contact World Relief:

Soviet Refugee Project
World Relief
P.O. Box WRC
Nyack, NY 10960
(914) 268-4135

You may also wish to contact EXODUS World Service, which
does good work providing information on refugee resettlement:

Dennis Ripley
EXODUS World Service
P.O. Box 7000
West Chicago, IL 60185-7000
(312) 733-8433

SOURCES

*F*or the sake of brevity, detailed footnotes and bibliography have not been included in this paperback condensation of *The Soviet Union on the Brink*. For a text which is three times the length of the present book, and for specific references for all citations and information included in the paperback, the reader is referred to *On the Brink*. However, I do want to give a brief summary of particularly important sources of information which have formed a basis for much of my research.

Pre-Gorbachev historical sections dealing with the Russian Orthodox church have relied heavily on Dmitry Pospielovsky, *The Russian Church under the Soviet Regime: 1917-82*, 2 vols. (Crestwood, N.Y.: St. Vladimir's Seminary Press, 1984) and Jane Ellis, *The Russian Orthodox Church: A Contemporary History* (Bloomington: Indiana University Press, 1986). Walter Sawatsky's *Soviet Evangelicals since World War II* (Scottdale, Penn.: Herald Press, 1981) is a landmark study of Protestants in the USSR. One of the reliable and readable sources of information for Soviet history in general is Mikhail Heller and Aleksandr Nekrich, *Utopia in Power: The History of the Soviet Union from 1917 to the Present* (New York: Summit Books, 1986).

Information on changes affecting religion in the Gorbachev period has often been based on *Keston News Service* (biweekly), Keston's *Religion in Communist Lands* (quarterly), and Michael Bourdeaux's *Gorbachev, Glasnost and the Gospel* (London: Hodder and Stoughton, 1990). Bourdeaux is the head of the Keston College research center, and a slightly revised U.S. paperback edition of his book is being released under the title *The Triumph of the Gospel over Communism* in mid-1991 by Bethany House Publishers (Minneapolis).

The excellent coverage of developments in the Soviet Union as found in *Report on the USSR* (weekly, Radio Free Europe) has been invaluable, as have the materials from Foreign Broadcast Information Service and Joint Publications Research Service, both located in Washington, D.C.

Numerous other books, publications, scholars, and newsletters and information from a wide variety of organizations involved with work in the USSR have been indispensable in the writing of this work. Finally, much of the information has come from personal interviews and research in the Soviet Union.